The
Good News
from
North Haven

The Good News from North Haven

Michael·L·Lindvall

DOUBLEDAY

New York • *London* • *Toronto* • *Sydney* • *Auckland*

PUBLISHED BY DOUBLEDAY
a division of Bantam Doubleday Dell Publishing Group, Inc.
666 Fifth Avenue, New York, New York 10103

DOUBLEDAY and the portrayal of an anchor with a dolphin
are trademarks of Doubleday,
a division of Bantam Doubleday Dell Publishing Group, Inc.

"The Christmas Pageant" and "Christmas Baptism" originally
appeared in the December 1987 and December 1990 issues of
Good Housekeeping.

Calligraphy by Anita Karl

Library of Congress Cataloging-in-Publication Data

Lindvall, Michael L., 1947–
  The good news from North Haven/by Michael L. Lindvall.
—1st ed.
    p.   cm.
    1. Christian fiction, American.   2. Minnesota—Fiction.
I. Title.
PS3562.I51266G6   1991
813'.54—dc20   91-10928
CIP
ISBN 0-385-41640-7

10 9 8 7 6 5 4 3 2 1

For my wife Terri,
who was unfailing in her support

Acknowledgments

To everyone who ever told me a story I offer my gratitude and apologies. Bits and pieces of a dozen tales have found their way onto these pages. My hope is that even though I have woven fiction from threads of true stories, I have managed to make up tales that tell the truth half as well as life does.

To everyone who ever listened to me tell a story I offer my gratitude and apologies: to my family who never seem to tire of listening, to a congregation that laughs in the right places, to supportive friends who told me to write a book.

I offer my appreciation to Garrison Keillor, Fred Craddock, and others who reminded me that stories are truer and infinitely more memorable than mere ideas.

Contents

Does the fish soar to find the ocean,
The eagle plunge to find the air—
That we ask the stars in motion
If they have rumour of thee there?

—Francis Thompson

For where two or three are gathered in my name,
there am I in the midst of them.

—Matthew 18:20 (Revised Standard Version)

The
Good News
from
North Haven

Introduction

North Haven

This is our fourth winter in North Haven, which is a curious name for the place. It's not clear what it's north of, other than most all of the continental United States. There is no "South Haven," nor even a "Haven." The name suggests a harbor and the proximity of water, which there was before the Cottonwood River altered its course. Now the river itself is a mile away and the old riverbed is a slough on the edge of town.

It takes about an hour to drive to Mankato, the nearest town of any size. From there it's another hour to Minneapolis–Saint Paul, "the Cities" to everybody here, as if there were no others. Interstate 90 passes well to the south. That and the river lend to the town an impression of a place that has been passed by. Annie and I never dreamed we'd live somewhere so far away. When we first came to town, people would say to us, "You know, Pastor, this isn't the end of the world. . . ." Then they'd hesitate and chuckle. "But from our front porches we can see it."

I am the pastor of Second Presbyterian Church. There is no First Presbyterian in town and there hasn't been for years. More than a century ago, the newly founded First—and then only—Presbyterian Church enjoyed a fine church fight. Folks still tell the story of the Sunday in June when half the congregation walked out during the sermon and founded Second Presbyterian.

All memories agree as to what the fight was about: whether young women ought to lead discussions at Christian Endeavor meetings or keep a low profile and ask questions when they got home, as St. Paul seems to have counseled. What memories do not agree on is who was on what side. Some people now say that the Second Presbyterian group that left was in favor of women speaking at meetings, some say they were against it. Whatever the truth, everyone agrees that Second Presbyterian Church was squarely established on the firm foundation of an important principle, even if no one is now quite sure what that principle was.

First Church's building burned to the ground a few years after the split, and most people assumed that this was a sign. They had no fire insurance, not because they couldn't afford it, but because buying fire insurance for churches was seen by many in those days to be sure evidence of weak faith. If you truly trusted that God would guard and prosper His church, this reasoning went, you didn't second-guess Providence by wasting money on insurance against "acts of God." In fact, some argued that buying insurance might even "tempt the Lord thy God" and actually cause fires. Most First Church folks switched over to Second Church after the fire. But a handful of stalwarts refused to yield on a matter of Presbyterian principle and became Methodists.

It was an age of high principles and even higher hopes. The first settlers had arrived in the years just after the Civil War. They came from upstate New York, Pennsylvania, and Ohio. They were mostly Presbyterians and Methodists with English and Scotch-Irish names. The Swedes, mostly Lutheran, came later, but in greater numbers. They all came first, of course, for the land—rolling grassland with black soil two feet thick that had never been turned by a plow.

But they also came to found a city—not a village, but a great city. These were people who dreamed boldly of what was to come. They were people who understood themselves to be at the advancing edge of a beneficent tide of civilization and true religion rising westward over the continent. They engaged in a long debate about what to name the town. Among the most favored suggestions were "New Corinth" and "New Athens." These were names that married the two worlds that the civilizers of the age wished to emulate: that of the Bible and that of classical Greece.

They settled on New Haven, not that there was an old Haven, but because "haven" is such a welcoming word and it seemed a less prideful name. People say that the "New" became "North" after the first winter, the surprising harshness of which impressed upon the settlers the northerliness of their new home. Winters are hard, of course, but it is more their length that dominates life here. Annie said to me just the other day that what she likes most about Minnesota weather is the almost guaranteed white Christmases. What she doesn't like is the white Easters. I am most impressed by the sharp distinction of the seasons. Each has a strong personality that dominates the mood of the place for the length of its stay. Life moves with the seasons here, much more so than in places less attached to land and blessed with a moderate climate.

The town fathers laid out North Haven on a grid. The streets running north and south were named after Presidents, in order of their tenures. The avenues running east and west were named after the states in alphabetical order. Today the streets stop with Grant, and the last avenue is Indiana. Most of them just end at a field on the edge of town. If I stand in the middle of Adams Street in front of our manse, I can turn north and see the wind moving in the corn where the street ends, and turn south and see the heat rising off the soybean field where the asphalt stops at the other end. The Main Street business district is four blocks long and is dominated by the Lyric Odeon Theatre in the middle, the Skelly gas station on one end, and the towering Farmers' Union grain elevators at the other. There is a drugstore, a coffee shop, a Woolworth's, Emma's

Notions 'n Stuff, the Red Owl grocery store, and the Blue Spruce Bar and Grille. There are also half a dozen empty storefronts.

Recent years have been unkind to the fond hopes of the past. It's a lament sung by many little towns in this part of the world. Farms are bigger, and with mechanization it takes fewer people to run them. Good roads have brought larger places closer. There is just not enough work. Young people leave. Few of those who go off to college return.

Those who stay do not despair, but they worry. They worry that they, too, may have to leave. The vision of a great city that so animated their great-grandparents came to be realized in other former villages, like Chicago and Minneapolis. But many of the great-grandchildren of those dreamers would not now choose to live in such proud places.

Second Presbyterian Church is small. It has two thirds the members it had a generation ago. The church sits on the corner of Main and Jefferson. It's a white frame building with a disproportionately small steeple. When I remarked on this to someone, I was told that the building committee had instructed the architect to make sure that the steeple was shorter than the town's water tower, so that lightning would strike the tower and not the church. It was a prudent plan. Lightning does strike the water tower and has never once hit the church. But the steeple looks too short.

The congregation's pastors mostly come fresh

out of seminary. Usually they grew up in large suburban churches. They stay about three years and return to the world they know better. They often come with hopes to do very grand things.

My predecessor in the pulpit was here only two years. On his last Sunday he preached a sermon on the fourteenth chapter of the Book of Exodus in which he represented himself as Moses and the congregation as the Children of Israel, a "stiff-necked people" reluctant to be led out of Egypt into the Promised Land of Canaan. By Canaan he meant, of course, his vision for Second Presbyterian Church. When he finished the sermon, he took off his pulpit robe, laid it over his arm, and walked down the aisle and out of the church. He and his wife got in their car and drove off, skipping the farewell reception the Women's Association had arranged in the Fellowship Hall. Such rudeness mystified these good people. But the sermon escaped them altogether, for it has always been clear to them where Canaan is—the rolling grasslands of southwestern Minnesota.

Four years ago, my wife Annie and I and our two children, Jennifer and Christopher, then nine and three, came here with our fond hopes. We are both children of the suburbs. We came partly out of an urban arrogance that fancied we could bring something to "these people." We came partly because we were romanced by a nostalgic vision of small-town life. We came mostly because it was the first place that would have us and we needed the job.

What we have found is a little less than we expected and a great deal more. The little less was the realization that people here and anywhere are just people, often stiff-necked, a little vain, a little jealous, and a little afraid. The great deal more has come in witnessing grace at work, so gently and surprisingly, in these same people. One can see it in any place where people live together, but in a small place like this, where life moves a bit more slowly, you see it more easily. It comes simply, in the "things that happen," in daily dramas that you come to recognize as tales of grace.

The Christmas Pageant

The Christmas Pageant is over. It was, in the end, wonderful, and now that it is past, my blood pressure and, in fact, the church's communal blood pressure, has dropped about twenty points. We got through it again without schism and with no divorces. None of the kids got grounded this year, but it was close.

The whole saga of the Christmas Pageant really began precisely forty-seven Christmases ago when Alvina Johnson first directed Second Presbyterian's "Children's Christmas Pageant," something that she continued to do through ten pastors, nine U.S. Presidents, three wars, and who knows how many Christian Education Committees, for the next forty-six years, but not this year, and that's the story. International alliances came and went; wars were fought and peace made; ministers were called and then called away—but Alvina Johnson directing the Children's Christmas Pageant was like a great rock in a turbulent sea.

Alvina is "Mrs. Johnson," although there is no "Mr. Johnson." There was a Mr. Johnson for only three and a half weeks, forty-nine years ago. A few days shy of their month's wedding anniversary, Mr. Johnson (nobody remembers his first name) left, although Alvina never puts it that way. She prefers to say, "He just ran off to Minneapolis," with the accent on *Minneapolis,* as if it were that notorious place and Mr. Johnson's morally feeble nature that lured him away from wife and home rather than anything having to do with Alvina.

Nobody here ever talks about why he left. They all know, just as they know why rain falls down and grass grows up. One might call Alvina "stubborn," but that word isn't quite enough. Alvina is intractable, intransigent, unmovable. This, everybody assumes, Mr. Johnson easily discovered in the space of three and a half weeks. When folks around here get put out with Alvina, who is disguised as a sweet and demure seventy-year-old lady, they refer to her, under their breath of course, as "the iron butterfly."

But Alvina does what she says, always, exactly, and forever. Forty-seven years ago somebody asked her to do the Christmas Pageant. She said yes. They didn't say, "Would you do the Christmas Pageant this year?" so Alvina, who is a literalist in all things, assumed that they meant forever, and she is a woman of her word.

Alvina's Pageants always had precisely nine characters: one Mary, one Joseph, three Wise Men, two Shepherds, one Angel, and one Narrator.

The script was simply the Christmas story out of the King James Bible, which meant that two six-year-old shepherds had to learn to say, "Let us now go even unto Bethlehem, and see this thing which is come to pass, which the Lord hath made known unto us."

Auditions for the nine parts were held the last Sunday afternoon in October for forty-six years. Rehearsals for the nine lucky winners were held for the next five Sunday afternoons. Alvina's goal was nothing less than perfection in Christmas pageantry: perfect lines, perfect pacing, blocking, enunciation, perfect everything, which is not easily achieved with little children, even nine carefully selected ones. Critics said that Alvina would have much preferred working with nine midget actors, if she could have gotten away with it.

Time and again people tried to get Alvina to open things up so that every kid who wanted a part could have one. "Alvina," they would say, "Scripture says that there was a heavenly host, not just one lonely angel. Alvina, why not a few more shepherds, then everybody could be in the Pageant?" or "Alvina, if there were shepherds, there had to be sheep, right? We'll make some cute little woolly sheep outfits for the three- and four-year-olds." "Nope," she'd answer, "too many youngsters, too many problems."

Early in the fall, however, something happened that deflected the inertia of nearly half a century of always doing it the way it had always been done. The Christian Education Committee included the three young mothers of last year's rejected Mary, Joseph, and Wise Man Number Two. And these young mothers pulled off what they call in Central America a *coup d'état*. At their September meeting they passed the following motion: "Resolved: All children who wish to be in the Christmas Pageant may do so. Parts will be found."

Alvina heard about it that night and was in my office the next morning at nine o'clock sharp. She began by asking me if I thought the decorations on the Christmas tree in the church parlor were appropriate. I had not noticed them, I said. Well, she informed me, they were walnut shells decorated to look like little mice with tiny stocking caps on their heads. "What," she asked, "do mice have to do with the birth of our Lord?"

Now, I knew this wasn't the problem. I, too, had heard about the committee meeting the night before. "What's the matter, Alvina?" I asked. "Young mothers," she said. She spit these two words out as though "young mother" were an illicit occupation. "Young mothers," she continued, "who have no knowledge of or experience in the proper direction of a Christmas Pageant. Young mothers are behind those walnut-shell mice and they are behind the destruction of the Christmas Pageant." She then resigned as director and said, "If these young mothers know so much, let them try to do it." She was angry, maybe even angry enough to quit the church and become a Methodist, but she didn't. I suspect that she wanted to hang around at least long enough to see the young mothers fall flat on their faces.

The Pageant was last week. The young mothers didn't fall flat on their faces, but the Pageant was, well, different from what everybody had come to expect over the last forty-six years. It seemed as though there were a cast of thousands, even though the actual number was fifty or so, which was every kid in the church up to about eighth grade. At this age, they would sooner die than get dressed up in their father's bathrobe and pretend to be a biblical character.

There must have been a dozen shepherds and ten angels (a veritable heavenly host). Then there were the sheep, a couple dozen three-, four-, and five-year-olds who had on woolly, fake-sheepskin vests with woolly hoods and their dads' black socks pulled up on their arms and legs. The Pageant was a lot of things, but smooth it wasn't. And one of the chief problems was these very sheep. Now, in suburban Christmas Pageants, I imagine sheep are well behaved and fairly quiet, but suburban kids have seldom seen real sheep. The only sheep most suburban kids have ever seen are on the front of Sunday church bulletin covers: peaceful, grazing sheep who just stand there and look cute and cuddly.

Half of the kids here live on farms. They've seen real sheep, many of them. They know that sheep don't just stand there. They know that sheep don't often follow directions. They know that sheep are dumb. They know that all sheep want to do is eat.

So, when the young mothers casually instructed the two dozen sheep to act like sheep, they really should have known better. Some of the sheep started to do a remarkable imitation of grazing behind the communion table. Some wandered over by the choir to graze, and others went down the center aisle. Some of them had donuts they found in the church parlor to make their grazing look even more realistic. When one of the shepherds tried to herd them a bit with his shepherd's crook, some of the sheep spooked and started to scatter just like real sheep do. Everybody knows that's how sheep act. It was, in fact, a remarkable imitation of sheep behavior, even though a bit out of the ordinary for a Christmas Pageant.

Now, Alvina was watching all this from the last pew of the sanctuary. I could just see her from where I was sitting. As the sheep spooked and scattered with much imitation bleating, Alvina looked down to hide a smirk. *Young mothers,* I'm sure she was thinking. *If they know so much, let them try to direct the Christmas Pageant.* The real climax of imprecision came, however, at that point of high drama when Mary and Joseph enter, Mary clutching a baby doll in a blue blanket. This year's Mary, whose name was actually Mary, was taking her role with an intense and pious seriousness. She looked into the face of the doll in her arms with eyes that really seemed to see the infant Christ. Joseph was another story. He had gotten the part because he had been rejected from Christmas Pageant participation by Alvina Johnson more times than any other kid in church. "With good reason," some might say.

Anyway, Mary and Joseph were to walk on as the Narrator read, "And Joseph also went up from Galilee, out of the city of Nazareth, into Judea, unto the city of David, which is called Bethlehem . . . to be taxed with Mary his espoused wife, being great with child." At least this is what the Narrator was *supposed* to read. It was what the Narrator had read at the rehearsal. But a few hours before the performance, one of the young mothers had observed that none of the children could much understand King James English, so they voted, in their ongoing mood of revolutionary fervor, to switch to the Good News translation of the Bible for the performance. "What kid knows what 'great with child' means?" they asked.

The Good News translation is much more direct at this point. So, as Mary and Joseph entered, the Narrator read, "Joseph went to register with Mary who was promised in marriage to him. She was pregnant."

As that last word echoed from the Narrator through the PA system into the full church, our little Joseph, hearing it, froze in his tracks, gave Mary an incredulous look, peered out at the congregation, and said, "Pregnant? What do you mean, pregnant?" This, of course, brought down the house. My wife, wiping tears from her eyes, leaned over to me and said, "You know, that may well be just what Joseph actually said."

Alvina was now wearing a look that simply broadcast *I told you so.* But as the Pageant wound into its closing tableaux and the church lights were dimmed for the singing of "Silent Night," a couple of magical—I would allow, miraculous— things happened. The sheep, when they had finished with their part, bleated their way down the aisle to sit in the last couple of pews to watch the end of the Pageant. Alvina was in the last pew and she suddenly found herself surrounded by a little herd of three-, four-, and five-year-olds in sheep outfits.

It was late, the church was warm, and the sheep were drowsy. I glanced over to Alvina as the Wise Men were exiting and the organ was softly playing the melody of "Silent Night." The sheep in the pew on either side of Alvina had fallen asleep and were resting their fake-wool heads on her shoulders, something they would feel comfortable doing with any grown-up in church. As the church went dark for the singing of "Silent Night," we could see what had been happening outside for the last hour. The first real snow of the winter was falling. Big, fat flakes floated down and covered everything with a white, uniform perfection. As we—little kids and grown-ups—saw it, there was a spontaneous and corporate "ahh."

We sang: "Silent night, holy night, All is calm, all is bright." It was very softly that we sang and all the sheep were quiet, even the ones who were awake, and everybody looked at the snow. It was as if flakes of grace were falling, falling free out of heaven and blessing the muddy earth with purity, a whiteness covering the dirt and the shoddiness with perfection. When the carol was finished, no one stirred for a long time. It wasn't planned, but we all just sat there and watched.

It seemed like an eternity, but it was maybe two minutes. Minnie MacDowell broke the spell. She's hard of hearing and always talks too loud. She meant to whisper to her husband, but everybody heard. "Perfect," she said, "just perfect."

And so it was—not perfect in the way Alvina's Pageants tried to make things perfect, but perfect in the way God makes things perfect. God accepts our fumbling attempts at performance, at love and fairness, and then covers them with grace. I think the moment may have even touched the iron butterfly. Minnie said that Alvina mentioned to her that if they needed any more sheep outfits for next year, she could perhaps find time to make a few.

The Little Things

The coming of our fourth winter in North Haven has been for me like a clock striking the hour. One, two, and three made a set, a time-trinity, but this fourth has drifted upon me whispering: "Long time, now, long time." This mood also has something to do with having turned forty in the fall. My thirties, I argued, were "mature youth." The actuarial tables gave me more distance ahead of me than behind. But forty is most likely halfway home, give or take a few years. Forty is second base: The pitcher is lined right up with home plate. One base behind, one base ahead.

It is a perch from which one is inclined to do some reconnoitering. Forty years lived and four of them in this one place and what difference has it all made? Second Presbyterian Church has a net membership of two fewer souls than four years ago. There are four more children registered in the Sunday school. I have preached 187 sermons here, baptized 8 babies and 1 middle-aged lady. I have married 17 couples and buried 28 people.

At current pace, that means over the next

twenty-five years: 1,175 more sermons, 50 more babies, 6 middle-aged ladies, 104 happy couples, and 175 funerals, not counting mine. Is anybody keeping track? And if all this is being tallied in some cosmic computer, will my file be distinguishable from that of a million other well-meaning clergy who worked hard enough and did a pretty good job?

As I sat in my study on a Tuesday morning after working out those chilling numbers on my pocket calculator, I glanced out the window at the snow from the storm of two weeks ago, now plowed into a dirty-brown wall around the perimeter of the parking lot. I turned to open my mail, every last piece of it third class. A minister's desk is deluged daily with promotional mailings from a zillion little companies out to sell you everything from large-print, red-letter Bibles to disposable communion cups. And a lot of them seem to be selling advice. They don't call it that. They call it "consulting," or "stewardship enrichment," or "educational enhancement," or "mission invigoration." I suspect that most of these outfits are run out of their basements by ministers who had done what I did and computed how many sermons they had yet to preach and determined it was time for them to do some income enrichment and career invigoration.

I usually throw these letters away unopened. But some savvy promoter suspected I would do that and he had printed in bright orange letters across the face of the envelope itself the hook that snagged my weak flesh. "Open This Envelope," it said, "and Revolutionize Your Church's Life and Mission." So I opened it and read the letter that began, "Dear Fellow Pastor." The word "new" appeared seven times in the text, the word "vigor" twice, and variations of the word "energy" four times. It told of a program replete with study books, special worship services, cassette tapes, and a leader's guide, all for $89.95, with a 10 percent discount for prepaid orders.

It seemed solid stuff, a little gimmicky maybe, but theologically grounded, and, well, "new," and "vigorous," and full of "energy." As I reached to set the letter aside, I saw that my calculator was still on the desk in front of me displaying the number "175," the number of projected funerals of my career. As I looked at those LCD numerals, they suddenly seemed a cryptic omen foreboding a career punctuated by nothing more lasting than a string of funerals. I checked the little box that said "Yes! I want to invigorate my church."

In the days before the materials arrived, the whole undertaking developed a sort of fantasy life for me. I imagined people in town saying to each other six months from now, "Boy, things are really hoppin' over to the Presbyterian church." I imagined the word circulating among ministers in nearby towns about the exciting growth in the North Haven church. I imagined my smiling photo on the religion page of the Mankato paper under the headline VISIONARY PASTOR AWAKENS SLEEP-

ING CHURCH. I even chose a title for the book I would write about it, *The North Haven Story.*

The *Pastor's Manual* for the Congregational invigoration Plan was not divided into anything as mundane as chapters. Rather, it consisted of six "Invigoration Steps." The first was entitled: "How to Get Your Church Board on Board." I did everything it said I should do, and the Session looked at me as if I had two heads and said: "Well, that might be nice. Go ahead, Dave, we won't stand in your way."

Invigoration Step One concluded with these words of advice: "Now that your church board is filled with excitement about the plan, your next step is to broaden this enthusiasm to the whole congregation through the Grand Kick-Off Dinner." The arrangements for this event were thoroughly outlined in Invigoration Step Two.

We had the Grand Kick-Off Dinner last Friday night. Including my wife and three members of the Ladies Aid Society who come to everything at church no matter what it is, a total of twelve people came. Historically, this was an interesting attendance figure, but a very disappointing beginning. We all had plenty to eat, however.

Invigoration Step Two ended with these words: "Now that real anticipation is brewing throughout the congregation, the moment has come to preach the sermon you have always meant to preach!" Step Three consisted of three suggested outlines of "the sermon you have always meant to preach" along with about a dozen "time-tested" illustrations.

I chose "Invigoration Sermon Outline B" and spent the better part of a week writing and rewriting a finely crafted piece of pulpit oratory. When the day came, I preached it well, although as the words came from my lips they sounded strangely unlike anything that I might ever really say. After the service, as the congregation filed through the greeting line on their way to the coffee hour, I waited expectantly for sermon reactions with less nonchalance than usual. The first person to offer anything beyond the usual pleasantries was Angus MacDowell, who said, "Fine sermon, Dave. Minnie and I have always liked that sermon, especially the part about the Lord not having any hands but our hands and any feet but our feet. Hadn't heard that since Reverend Willis back in the fifties."

As I settled into the living room couch that afternoon, I came to understand that I was being kindly humored by a congregation that was quite as vigorous as it had any desire to be. Sunday afternoons, after the peak of morning worship, are usually a spiritual valley, but that one was deeper than usual. From it, everything I'd ever done in my ministry was shaded to look like a series of fumbles and small-time blunders. This last one was symbolic of them all. One day I would step across home plate, pass from the field, and in no time drop right out of the world's memory. Any squeak I had made in history would soon be silenced out.

The little wake that trailed my stern would soon smooth over.

A crazy childhood memory dropped into my head that seemed a dark parable for life itself. When I was six or seven, I faithfully watched a kids' TV show called *Axel's Tree House*. This was the early fifties: live, local programming, unrehearsed, unprofessional, and unpredictable. Axel was an old man, or at least I remember him as an old man. He was probably about forty. He lived in a tree house and spoke, for some inexplicable reason, with a fake Swedish accent. Two or three times during the show, Axel would look through a hand-held telescope and say, "I tink I see dem Little Rascals out dere." And behold, a Little Rascals adventure would appear on the screen.

At the beginning and the end of the show, the camera would pan to a small set of bleachers, ostensibly inside Axel's tree house, in which were seated Axel's "friends," about twenty-five cheering seven- to ten-year olds. Even then I wondered how so many people could fit into a tree house. The kids would cheer when the Little Rascals came on. They would laugh at Axel's jokes and appear stumped by his riddles. At the end of the program, Axel would take a microphone taped to a three-foot stick and ask if any of the kids would like to say hello to their family or their friends "out dere in TV land."

One day when Axel asked this question a kid about my age shot his hand in the air. Axel poked the microphone in front of the kid and the camera came full-face on the youngster. "Vat's your name?"

"Jimmy," the kid said.

"And vat vould you like to say?" asked Axel.

Jimmy didn't say anything at first. Then he smiled broadly, made a certain vulgar hand gesture directly into the lens of the camera and said, "This is for you, Herbie, and I really mean it."

Immediately the screen went black. It stayed black for about three minutes. When the show came back on, Axel started to interview the other kids, and tell jokes and ask riddles. Jimmy was gone. There was not even an empty spot in the bleachers where Jimmy had been. No one even mentioned Jimmy or what he had done. It was as if Jimmy had vanished from the earth, as if Jimmy had never existed. That's the core of the memory —not what Jimmy did, I had seen that small vulgarity before and was not shocked. What etched itself on my memory was the idea that a kid could just disappear like that without anybody saying anything about it.

I felt like a Jimmy that Sunday afternoon. Someday they were going to pull me right out of the bleachers and everybody would budge over to cover my spot. No mention would be made of my name. The show would go on as if I had never been there.

I couldn't abide my office the next Tuesday morning, so I went to get my hair cut. The town barber's name is Harry. He's about seventy and a chatty type with a repertoire of stale barber jokes. No pension, I suppose, so he keeps cutting hair. He's says he's "R.C.," but I don't think he's been in church for years. He starts every one of my haircuts with "I'm Catholic, but . . ." I think he says that so I won't ask him to come to church. Harry asked what kinds of things ministers did on the other six days of the week. He wasn't teasing —it was an honest question. I talked about meetings, hospital visits, and counseling with people who had problems to talk over.

Something I said touched a nerve in Harry and he started to talk. He talked about being a kid and what a pain it was. He started to talk about his father, whom he called "my old man." This seventy-year-old was calling his father "old man." My haircut was done; we were alone in the shop. A scissors in one hand and a comb in the other, he was resting them both on my shoulders as he talked. He talked about how his old man mercilessly beat him and his mother most every Saturday night. He talked about how afraid he was, about how much he loved and hated his father. He said he had never told anybody about this before, not in sixty years. His mother, he said, carried the secret to her grave. Nobody had ever guessed. We were both facing the big barbershop mirror. His eyes were reddening. We looked at each other in the mirror in a way we could not have face to face. I reached to my shoulders and held his hands, and said something about when you forgive somebody it doesn't mean that you are saying that what they did was all right.

That evening I had a meeting at church but got home fairly early. Annie said that the kids were waiting up for me and would be wanting their story and kisses. I was exhausted and would much sooner have dropped myself in front of the television. But I went upstairs and found two little peanuts fighting sleep. They had the book ready, a slip of yellow construction paper marking the spot where we had stopped reading the night before. So I read chapter six of *Ramona the Pest*. They fell asleep before its end. I kissed them both and sat at the edge of the bed for a moment and said their prayers for them.

And sitting there it came to me that of all the meetings I had attended in the last few days, of all the sermons I'd preached, of all the programs I'd introduced or tried to introduce, the most important things I had done in all my busy-ness were to touch Harry the barber's hands and to read chapter six of *Ramona the Pest*. These were important things—not because the other things were unimportant. They were important because the mark a man or a woman makes on this world is most often a trail of faithful love, and quiet mercies, and unknown kindnesses.

Merciful Snow

Nothing that would appear important seems to happen here. But in the rhythm of this gentler routine, outwardly insignificant events that once would not have held my attention for an hour receive an attention I have come to know they deserve. Our time is cut into segments by these small events: births, deaths, marriages, people moving to Florida, hot spells, and blizzards.

We write down our time markers in the *North Haven Herald,* the town's only newspaper, which is published weekly. It's a weekly except in the summer when Bud Jennerson, who writes, edits, sells the advertising, operates the press, and answers the phone, goes to Colorado for the month of July to visit his brother. Then, for a month, the *Herald* becomes a monthly.

Bud's journalistic eye surveys the whole range of life in this small place, ranging from malicious to petty to sentimental to genuinely noble. But the *Herald* reports only the stories that seem to Bud to be good for us to know more about than word of mouth is able to relate. Weddings, for instance, are reported in great detail. Bud's wedding stories routinely report the color of the bridesmaids' dresses, the central point of the minister's nuptial meditation, and the menu at the reception. And there is always a photograph: the bride in white looking pleased and so very young; the groom in a rented velvet tuxedo with sleeves a little too short. In many cases he sports the last tie he'll wear until his next formal occasion in life when he will be the subject of one of Bud's obits. Bud also reports the weather in great detail, although only after the fact. But he reports in detail, like who in town got water in their basements and how much.

Bud's most impressive literary achievements are his regulation length (three 4-inch columns) obituaries written about those lives about which there is precious little to say, or at least precious little that Bud can say in the newspaper. With consummate skill, he weaves all the expected words together to say little, which pleases everyone. The interpersonal and political realities of small-town life counsel equal-length obituaries. Obits of varying lengths and content would be a potential source of wounded family pride that might last generations and bring ire upon the tenuous operation of a one-man newspaper. So Bud chooses his words with a studied deliberateness. It is a studied deliberateness that I, as a writer of funeral eulogies, especially appreciate.

Last week's *Herald,* which was mailed out the Friday after the New Year, included an obit for an old woman, Priscilla Atterby, and a second-page feature about the blizzard that hit on Wednesday. For Bud and most of the town, these events were two more markers in time: "the year that old Mrs. Atterby died," or "the year we had the big storm right after New Year's." But for me, these two events wove themselves together in such a way that they became not just news, but news for me —oddly enough, "good news."

Priscilla Atterby died at eighty-four years: "four-score if by reason of strength," as the Psalmist has it. All of her life was lived here in North Haven. "Never saw the ocean till I was sixty-two," she told me once, and then allowed as to how she was really rather disappointed in it when she finally did see it. "Looked just like Lake Michigan," she said.

"But Priscilla," I countered, "on the other side of that ocean is France, thousands of miles away; it's only ninety miles across the lake to Wisconsin."

She then looked at me without a hint of humor and said, "But Reverend, you can't see either of them, so what does it matter?"

Priscilla was a world-class worrier. She worried most about her three children, who are themselves now grandparents. Each of them moved out of town right after marriage, partly, I suspect, to distance themselves from the immediate clutches of their mother's unrelenting concern. Two of them moved out to California. Priscilla worried about earthquakes. One moved to Chicago and Priscilla worried about crime and fire. "Fire?" I asked when she shared her anxiety with me during a pastoral call.

"What happened once can happen again," she answered.

Her face was deeply lined. People who knew her longer than I said that the worrying was something that had animated her only for the last twenty years or so. When she was younger it was something a bit different that drove her. "Agitation," somebody called it. "Priscilla always looked, well, agitated," this friend had said. I think the image was meant to be taken literally, like the agitator of an old Maytag wringer-washer, never sitting still, never letting anything be. It was, I suspect, Priscilla's agitated love that chased her daughters to California and her son to Chicago. It was this agitated love that slid into intrepid worry in old age.

During the funeral it started to snow, gently at first, and then very hard. The television had said that if this storm "swooped south, we might really get walloped." Newscasters everywhere seem bent on talking about winter weather in apocalyptic terms as if the same thing didn't happen every winter. On the other hand, folks here, being quite accustomed to it, try to outdo each other in being blasé about blizzards.

I, however, am possessed by an outlander's agitation about snow. My readiness to cancel everything at the sight of the first snowflake has become something of a standing joke in town. True to form, I had told a half-dozen people how worried I was that we wouldn't get Priscilla in the ground before the latest blizzard immobilized southwestern Minnesota.

I was reading the New Testament lessons when I first noticed the thick, heavy flakes through the funeral home window. The storm had "swooped south," I thought to myself. My minister's calendar-brain began to race ahead to everything in my life that the weather was going to foul up for the next couple of days: a meeting about the church's budget deficit, a Presbytery meeting over in Mankato where I was doing a big report, and the annual meeting of the congregation on Sunday after church. A worry lump began to congeal in my stomach. I was reading through the funeral service on automatic pilot when I realized the words from the fourteenth chapter of John's Gospel were bouncing from my eyes, out of my mouth, and into the ears of Priscilla Atterby's crowd of mourners: "Peace I leave with you, my peace I give unto you; not as the world giveth, give I it unto you. Let not your heart be troubled, neither let it be afraid."

Priscilla, I thought, *you never knew peace in this world. Yours was a troubled heart, anxious, thumping, rising to a start at every little threat to equilibrium.* But in funeral meditations, as in Bud's obits, you don't say everything that's on your mind. In prayer, we remembered Priscilla, for whom "the fever of life is over" and who now knew "peace at last," as Newman had prayed. Death, after eighty-four years, had stilled her troubled heart. Last night Minnie MacDowell had peered into the casket at Priscilla and said, predictably, "She looks so peaceful." That old mourner's euphemism appeared to be true in this case. Priscilla really did look to be at peace. The worry lines were relaxed from her face, her anxious eyes now peacefully closed. With a word, God was able to convince her of the simple truth that a lifetime of cajoling by her late husband and three children had never brought her to, namely that "everything is gonna be all right, Priscilla, everything is gonna be all right, Mom."

We sang "Abide with Me," got in our cars, and drove very slowly to the cemetery. We walked up a long, shallow hillside to the open grave, a warm black cave in the blinding white of the snow, and there we laid Priscilla Atterby. I went straight home afterward, somehow feeling good for her, but in a dither about how the snow might foul up the next few days of my life. It snowed all that day and night and most of the next day. Then for two more days the wind howled and screamed. The old manse we live in trembled before the power of it. When the storm was over, it was as though the town had entered another level of a many-tiered reality, a sculptured sea of frozen white waves curving over cars. Parabolas were carved around the trunk of each tree in mathematical perfection. Snow arched up to the eaves on the east side of every house. All was white, all except the sky, which was a blue intense beyond description.

We were snowbound—literally bound by the

snow for four days. Everything stopped: school, meetings, work for most everybody except the plow operators and the mailmen following in their swath. My agitation built and then crested on the second day when it became obvious that more than half of a week was going to be plucked right out of my calendar. I canceled meetings and fretted over what was not going to get done, all of it seeming so essential. Everybody agreed that we'd had a "decent little storm" and that I had not been an alarmist. Those who remembered said it called to mind the great Armistice Day blizzard of 1940. I felt somewhat vindicated.

When I informed a fellow clergyman over the phone that I could not make the committee meeting in Mankato, I heard a set of half-forgotten words tumble out of my mouth and onto the phone. "Milt," I said, "look at it this way, in a hundred years we'll all be dead." That piece of folk wisdom belonged to my late Uncle Paul, my mother's gangly bachelor brother, who could be counted on to say it every time something didn't go just the way he or somebody else had planned, which I recall as being fairly often.

After that remark there was, of course, nothing else to say, so I hung up and looked out the window at this white act of God that was in all its lumbering and relentless might foiling the plans and plottings of thousands of His creatures. "Be still." The words whispered invitingly to me. "Be still, and know that I am God." It is often so hard to hear such whispers in this life. Priscilla Atterby had known God, but had never been still, not until two days ago when God's love finally held her agitated soul in a quiet embrace.

This cold, irresistible embrace held us so tenaciously that we had to drop our armful of doings and makings and plannings and yield to stillness. It was a mandatory stillness that insisted we listen as it told us what we know but forget again and again. In tandem, the blizzard and Priscilla's death were an Epiphany epiphany. They were a manifestation of simple truth in the midst of outward uneventfulness insisting again that all our mortal effort, all our ambitions, all our worries, all our dreams, whether noble or vain, are as little before God, not so much because we are so small, but because God is so great. The blizzard was barely a whisper, as divine utterances go, but it was enough to still me and put before me again who God is and who I am.

The Ocarina Band

People's notions of what details are important enough to record in our church records have changed dramatically with the years. Session records of a hundred years ago, for instance, are long on descriptions of the spiritual condition of church members, individually and collectively. I came across this in the minutes of the Stated Meeting of June 1891: "Miss Elfreda Matson was again summoned before the Session and queries were put to her in a Gentle and Christian manner regarding certain reports of Intemperance." And this from the Session's October 1899 meeting. "It was felt by all that the recent Communion Season was marked by renewed concern for Spiritual Matters and many felt led to Commit themselves anew to the Work of Christ." Our Clerks of Session maintained the tradition of capitalization for emphasis long after it had passed from secular fashion. More recent minutes talk a lot about money (the lack of it) and church programs (always new).

Church members are no longer singled out By Name, nor is there much reflection about Spiritual Condition.

In the minutes of various Session meetings from 1919 to 1921 I found one of our more curious pieces of history—the story of the S.P.O.B., as the minutes usually abbreviated it, which stood for the "Second Presbyterian Ocarina Band." An ocarina I knew to be a once popular musical instrument about the size and shape of a sweet potato and yielding an airy sound like that of a recorder. The player blows into a mouth hole at one end and controls the pitch by covering and uncovering the finger holes on the side.

The first reference was from the minutes of the Session Meeting of February 1919:

A number of the boys of our church have proposed the founding of a Musical Band which would be composed of young men playing the ocarina. They suggested that the Band could accompany the congregation and organ in singing at Sunday Morning Services and perhaps present concerts of a Spiritual Nature on special occasions. The band would be under the direction of Mr. Angus MacDowell, a Junior student in the North Haven High School, and would include boys aged fifteen through eighteen years. It was further suggested that Church Funds be used for the purchase of Nine Ocarinas.

The boys were dismissed with appreciation and there followed a long discussion of the Merits of such a Musical Band. Elder Anston noted that the ocarina was an instrument of Recent Invention and that there was no clear Biblical Mandate for such an innovation. The Rev. Mr. Wilson observed that the shape of the Flutes mentioned in Scripture is unknown and such Biblical instruments may well have resembled the modern ocarina as much as that instrument we call the Flute today. Elder Anston noted the Cost of the instruments and questioned the Steadiness and Determination of Boys to bring such an enterprise to fruition. But it was agreed that Certain Risks and Innovations may be necessary to insure the ongoing interest of Modern Young People in Religious Matters. The Session voted 5-1 for the Foundation of the Second Presbyterian Ocarina Band.

From the minutes of the Session Meeting of April 1919:

The pastor reported to the Session the many Favorable Comments offered to him by Members of the Congregation and Visitors regarding the S.P.O.B. Many in attendance observed that Volume, Life, and Interest were added to the singing in recent services of worship, most especially that of Easter Sunday. The boys' rendition of "Jesus Christ Has Risen Today" at the opening of that service called to the Minds of Many Worshipers the Very Spirit that must have been about on that first Easter Day. The Session voted 6-0 to purchase three additional ocarinas for new band members and 12copies of *Favorite Sunday School Songs (With Helpful Notes for Instruments)*.

From the minutes of the Session Meeting of January 1920:

Young Mr. Angus MacDowell, who directs the S.P.O.B., was in attendance to request of the Session that support be given from the Church for the purpose of purchasing Appropriate Uniforms for the Band. Such uniforms would not be Military in Nature, nor would they seek to call Undue Attention to the boys, rather they would provide a Pleasing and Uniform appearance to the ensemble in the church. It was noted that the band is now larger in number than the Church Choir and has developed a Following and Popularity, especially among young ladies, in the Larger Community. The Pastor observed that many Methodists and even Episcopalians had been in attendance at the Christmas Services featuring the Band. Mr. MacDowell informed the Session that he had received Numerous Requests for the band to perform in Other Churches and Worldly Gatherings, but these the boys had declined in deference to the admonition of the Shorter Catechism that "Man's chief end is to glorify God and enjoy Him forever." The Session voted 6–0 to make a contribution of $150 toward the purchase of Uniforms.

From the minutes of the Session Meeting of May 1920:

Elder Craddock reported that the Uniform Fund had been oversubscribed and that the excess monies had been used by the boys to purchase Other Instruments in addition to the traditional ocarina. Some in the band felt this would add Depth and Rhythm to the sound of the Band. He also noted that several young Methodist men had requested that they be permitted to join the S.P.O.B., as their congregation offered no such Opportunity. Other elders inquired of Elder Craddock as to whether these young Methodists understood clearly that the band's chief purpose was to contribute to the worship of Second Presbyterian. He said that they clearly understood this, but, he noted, many boys in the Band now looked to Expand the Horizons of the organization. The Session voted 6–2 to invite Methodist and Other Protestant young men to participate in the S.P.O.B.

From the minutes of the Session Meeting of October 1920:

Elder Anston reported that Reports to the effect that the S.P.O.B. had been engaged to perform at the Grand Army of the Republic's Annual Ball were Indeed True. Since the addition of Other Instruments, the Popularity of the Band had increased even further. Many boys, Elder Anston observed, seemed to take Undue Pride in their membership in the organization and to see ocarina music as an End in Itself. The Session voted 6–0 to request that the Pastor counsel with the Boys regarding the Purpose and Mission of their organization.

From the minutes of the Session Meeting of December 1920:

The Rev. Mr. Wilson reported that he held a Lengthy conversation with young Mr. Angus Mac-Dowell and other boys in the ocarina band regarding the Mission of that organization. It seems that Some Dissension has arisen in the group. Some members wish the band to continue to play primarily for Services of the Church. Others envision Greater Things, and note that the Gospel does not forbid Christians from performing Popular Music in Worldly Places. The pastor added that many parents have expressed Concern for the Welfare of their boys. The pastor expressed concern about the Ill Effects of Dissension in the Church over this matter.

For nearly a year, there was no mention in the Session minutes of the S.P.O.B. The next and last entry on the subject was from the meeting of September 1921. (A new clerk now keeps the minutes; he no longer uses capitalization for emphasis.)

The pastor noted with regret that he had been informed by Mr. Angus MacDowell of the recent dissolution of the ocarina band. The group had become very popular locally. Differing perspectives regarding purpose, musical interpretation, and frequency of rehearsals arose in the group. The band was often called upon to perform at sundry worldly gatherings. In such situations temptations were strong, and the boys yielded. The group became degenerate and voluntarily disbanded over the summer.

Degenerate! Yielded! I let the heavy old leather-bound minute book slap down flat on the desk. I had to call Angus, who is a pillar of the church and of rectitude in general. What do eighteen-year-old boys yield to? My first thought was, of course, eighteen-year-old girls, those ocarina band groupies who had been innocently mentioned in the minutes. Or maybe the unnamed temptation was drink. Home brew or bootlegged whiskey may well have found their way into the G.A.R. Annual Ball. I couldn't wait. I phoned Angus and asked if I could stop by with some old Session minutes that I had a question or two about.

"Those minutes don't tell the half of it, Dave." Angus began. "They don't tell the tenth of it.

Such a deal it was—the ocarina band." His memory of the events was undimmed by the years. In fact, time had sharpened his perspective.

"Oh, we thought we were hot stuff. Dark blue uniforms with red trim on the lapels and on the ends of the sleeves. How we strutted about. Every boy in town wanted in. And then every mother in town wanted her son in. Except it was only for the Presbyterians at first."

Minnie came in very slowly with three cups of coffee lapping over their brims and a plate of shortbread. Angus retrieved an album with some old S.P.O.B. pictures and set it on my lap. They were formal studio photographs: three rows of boys in sepia tone, the back row standing, the middle row on chairs and the front row on the floor. Each boy held what looked like a sweet potato, which is, in fact, the nickname for the instrument. If you didn't know, the picture looked like twenty-four boys in identical suits holding identical vegetables. The contrasting stripe running down the sleeves and pants legs of the boys' uniforms was just noticeable. Each young face bore a look of utter and concentrated seriousness. Angus pointed to the gangly boy holding a baton on the end of the last row. "That's me," he said, "the director." He chuckled as he tapped the picture of his young self with his old man's finger.

"Oh, Dave, it was such serious stuff. It was so important. We planned such big things. We worried and we got upset with each other. We got mad at the church. And our parents got into it and they worried what would happen if their son wasn't in the band, or what might happen if he was. And the church talked about the far-out worship ideas of the pastor what with 'sweet potatoes in church'! And the Session agitated about it. The whole town got wrapped up in it. And then it all fell apart."

It was about this "falling apart" that I wanted details. Angus knew what I had read and guessed at my curiosity. "Temptations were strong, and the boys yielded," he quoted. Minnie set down her coffee cup and looked curious. "Nothing like you're thinking, nothing so juicy," he continued. "In the end it was just money. The G.A.R. paid us for doing the Annual Ball. Twenty dollars. We took the money and divided it up. It was our first and last paying gig. Word got out that the ocarina band from the Presbyterian Church were musicians for hire, which put us in company where some mothers didn't want their boys. But it wasn't just about the money. Everybody had gotten so serious about it. There were big debates about whether we should play only hymns or if we could play dance tunes. And there were those who said the uniforms were too proud. There was lots of talk and lots of meetings. It all started to pull at us and after the G.A.R. Ball it just kinda came apart like things do."

I guess I was disappointed that the story ground to such a less than sensational end. But that's how it is, again and again. Human enterprises seem born with the seeds of their demise.

Our most strenuous efforts so often seem to develop a centrifugal force bent on pulling them apart. Truth is, the line separating vision from vanity, purpose from ego, determination from stubbornness, is very fine.

As I walked home, I had no trouble imagining the plans and the passions that had animated the short life of the S.P.O.B. I knew that there were days in those years when some people in this town thought of little else. Sixteen-year-old boys spent all day Saturday with an ocarina at their mouth trying to get "Onward, Christian Soldiers!" just right. I had no trouble imagining the heated discussions about the admission of "young Methodists." I could imagine the gravity of those Session meetings, the adamant opinions of parents and boys. I could imagine Angus a bit too proud. But I could also imagine the satisfaction so many had found in the airy, flute-like music of a couple dozen ocarinas playing sweet old hymns.

I could easily imagine all this because I know how matters as passing as ocarina bands occupy me and the people around me. Annie and I have been agonizing for three weeks over our Christopher's Little League team assignment. My congregation is currently animated by the question of whether or not to sing "Amen" at the end of every hymn or only hymns that are, properly speaking, prayers. My next-door neighbor, Bernie, is in a state over the grubs that are ruining his front lawn. These things will pass, and in seventy years will loom no larger than the matter of the ocarina band does now.

But the ocarina band *did* matter. And Little League matters. Amens to end hymns matter. Even Bernie's lawn matters. But how much? Most of us are tempted either to care far too much or to care hardly at all. Somewhere in between there lies the place of proper concern. In this place you are free to be passionate and engaged. But from this place you can see what it will all look like in seventy years.

The Affair

The Lyric Odeon Theatre and St. Peter's Lutheran Church are the most notable architectural achievements in town. Both were designed to evoke some place other than southwestern Minnesota. In the case of St. Peter's, which was built about the turn of the century, that some place else was southern Sweden, whence most of the church's members had come not too many years before. In the case of the Lyric Odeon, built in the late twenties, the some place else was Venice, where nobody here had ever been, but which everybody understood to be a great capital of culture where all things were beautiful. The theater sits on Main Street, a jewel of what is now called "Italian Baroque Revival" sandwiched between two plain and dour red brick storefronts. Each year a handful of architectural aficionados journey to North Haven to view the Lyric Odeon and to say to us again, "Do you *know* what a treasure you have here?" It is a question that grates in its implication that people in a town like this could not possibly know.

The Lyric Odeon barely survived the advent of television in the fifties and is now just barely surviving the challenge of home videos. Truth is, by the time movies get to the Lyric Odeon, they are usually already out on video. But enough people seem willing to spend the extra couple of bucks to see a movie at the theater rather than at home. They justify the expense, they say, because "there's nothing like the big screen." This may be true, but there's more to it. Watching a movie is an altogether different experience when you are doing it with a few dozen other people than at home with one or two, or none.

People also go to the movies instead of watching home videos because they just want to get out of the house—which is why Jimmy Wilcox went alone to see *Lethal Weapon II* in the middle of March at the Lyric Odeon. Ardis, his wife, had spent another dinner talking about how they "don't communicate anymore." When he asked her after dinner to go to the movies, Jimmy knew Ardis would say no. She hates violent movies and would never go to anything with a title like *Lethal Weapon II.* "You don't mind if I go alone, do you?" he asked.

"Not in the least," she replied, and tossed the wet sponge she had used to wipe up the table all the way across the kitchen into the sink. Ardis knew Jimmy knew that she would say no.

Jimmy sat halfway down and a few seats into the right side of the center section of the Lyric Odeon. For a time, he was the only person in his row. He didn't notice Sharlette Wiggins and her sister, Ginny, when they sat down a few seats to his left; nor did he see the Lindsoes, who sat on the other end of the row.

Jimmy is in his mid-thirties and has been putting on weight. Ever since his senior year in high school and until sometime this past year, his pant size had been a 32-inch waist, 30-inch inseam. It had been an unhappy day when he told Ardis that she'd better order the new slacks she was going to send for from Monkey Ward's in a 34-inch waist. The three pairs that soon arrived were all Jimmy wore anymore, even though all the old pairs of 32's were still in the closet. He kept them because, he said to himself, he would start to "watch it" (meaning what he ate) and maybe even jog in the mornings before he went into the store.

But the morning of the day Jimmy went to see *Lethal Weapon II,* all three pairs of 34's were in the wash at the same time. He put on one of the more generously cut 32's, sucked in his gut, snapped the snap, zipped up the fly, and said half aloud, "Not bad."

"Not bad" until he sat down, that is. Jimmy spent most of the afternoon at his desk going over invoices. When he finally got sufficiently uncomfortable, he did what most of us over thirty have done at one time or another. He undid his belt, unbuttoned the button, and unzipped his fly halfway.

When he sat down in the Lyric Odeon that evening, he was even more uncomfortable than he

had been in the afternoon. At dinner he had
wolfed down Ardis's mashed potatoes with ruta-
baga and two large pieces of potato sausage. The
size 32 slacks that had been "not bad" in the
morning and a little too tight in the afternoon
were now excruciatingly uncomfortable. Ten minutes into the movie, Jimmy figured everybody was
watching Mel Gibson pretty closely and wouldn't
notice, so he did what he had done at the office
that afternoon: he unbuckled, unbuttoned, unzipped, and sat back to watch the movie in comfort.

Nobody would have noticed, of course, except
that about three quarters of the way through the
movie Sharlette decided that she really did want
popcorn after all. She went to the right, as providence would have it, and said, "Excuse me,
Jimmy," when she was about two seats away.
(They graduated from high school together.)
Jimmy should have stayed in his seat and squeezed
his legs to the side to let Sharlette by. This is what
Jimmy said he should have done. But now that it's
all over, I'm not so sure.

What Jimmy did was to stand up. Not until he
began to stand did he remember that his pants
were unbuckled, unbuttoned, and unzipped. Perhaps he should have just held them up as Sharlette
passed by. This is what Jimmy told me he should
have done. But again, I'm not so sure. What he
did do was buckle, button, and zip as fast and
discreetly as he could. Jimmy was almost quick
enough. Sharlette noticed nothing until she felt

the tug on her skirt where Jimmy's zipper was stuck. "Just a minute, Sharlette!" Jimmy whispered as he furiously tugged at the zipper. She assumed that Jimmy, for some curious reason, was holding on to her skirt. "Jimmyyyy," she giggled, "let go a' me!"

In no time the folks in the rows behind were politely asking them if they could "please sit down so we can see the movie." The zipper was intractable, Jimmy didn't want to rip Sharlette's dress, so he told her in a few whispered words what the problem was. This, however, only made her giggle more uncontrollably. They walked out of the Lyric Odeon in an odd and intimate tandem with Jimmy holding one hand around Sharlette to steady her while his other hand held up his pants. They whisked through the lobby, onto Main Street, and into the alley that separates the Piggly Wiggly from the dime store. There, after many apologies, Jimmy finally managed to extricate himself from Sharlette, who seemed to think it all riotously funny. As they came back into Main Street, the theater was just emptying out. Mel Gibson had foiled the South African drug smugglers, and everybody was going home.

Jimmy still speculates that it would have been nothing more than "one of life's embarrassing moments" had not Sharlette acted the way she did. Sharlette and Ginny, he explained, are Friday night fixtures at the Blue Spruce Bar and Grille. Friday nights are given over to the "All U Can Eat Fish Fry" and the "All U Can Drink Special of the

Night." That night, Sharlette told Jimmy in the alley as explanation of her inability to maintain her composure, the Special of the Night had been Tequila Sunrises, which she especially liked. "I remember back in high school," Jimmy would later tell me, "Sharlette Gunderson—that was her maiden name—just giggled when she drank. She used to giggle till she wet her pants."

Jimmy guesses that at least two dozen people saw them leave the theater together. He says he caught Danny Olson's wide eyes as he and Sharlette flew through the lobby and he also has a hunch that somebody may have seen them in the alley. "It was dark, but not that dark," he said worriedly.

A few weeks after all this happened, Jimmy called the church office and asked for an appointment for the next day. He came in promptly at ten, sat down in the chair opposite the desk in my study, and said straight out, "Ardis suggested I come in and set you straight before you heard anything."

"David," he said while shaking his head incredulously, "you need to know that Sharlette Wiggins and I are not having an affair." Annie had told me a few nights before that she had heard just that at a PTA meeting. Jimmy related the story of the zipper with all the attention to detail of a well-rehearsed defense witness. I could imagine him telling it to Ardis, as I am sure he has more than once. "The rumors have got Ardis and Mom all upset," he said, "and we thought you needed to know the truth."

Rumors, of course, are especially sharp swords in a small town. I ached for Jimmy. There are few things more infuriating than to be falsely accused. Every protestation of innocence sounds suspect. (Would an adulterer hesitate to lie?) So as we sat in my study I shared Jimmy's indignation. We shook our heads and lamented "what gossip like this can do to folks." Truth is, I think Sharlette had been quenching the fires of rumor by giggling out the zipper story over Tequila Sunrises at the Blue Spruce. When our conversation fell into a moment of silence, Jimmy suddenly slapped his knees and uttered one of those drawn-out "weeell's" that mean, "I think I'm going to leave now—maybe." But he didn't get up to go.

"How's Ardis doing with all of this," I asked. "If she needs an ear, tell her to stop by."

"Oh, Ardis," Jimmy sighed. He hesitated for a moment, looked at the door, and then looked at me. "We should both probably come in to talk one of these days. We've been having some problems, I mean long before the Sharlette business."

His tale was familiar enough. Marriage after sixteen years had gone stale. His work was a bore. Everything was suddenly old. Ardis was always harping about "communication" and reading him articles out of *Redbook* like "Refreshing Your Marriage" while he was trying to watch "The Terminator" on TV. "It was getting bad," he confessed.

"And now?" I asked.

"Well, it's funny," he answered. "Since the Sharlette thing, we sort of turned a corner. When the rumors started to fly and Ardis heard them, she was ready to call the lawyer. She came to me in a fury and I told her the zipper story and she said, 'Ya, right!' and spent that night at her mother's. I guess she spent the night thinking about us. Later she told me that she was ready to forgive me, but her mother said that before she did that she should call Sharlette and tell her off. Of course Sharlette told her the zipper story and giggled so much that Ardis figured it had to be true.

"When LaMont first told me that rumors were out about me having an affair, I was furious. Then a funny thing happened." Jimmy lowered his head and voice to indicate that he was going to reveal an even greater confidence. "Then I started to think: 'What would it be like to have an affair, not with Sharlette, of course, but maybe an affair in Minneapolis? What would it be like to be with somebody else all the time? What would it be like to get divorced from Ardis? And how about the kids?' I swear, Pastor, I had never even thought about having an affair until I heard that I was already having one. When I thought about it, it scared me to death. The picture in my head of what it would be like if it were really true made me think a lot. I really do love Ardis."

Which is why I say that it was maybe a good thing that Sharlette went to the right to get popcorn and that Jimmy stood up to let her by. Who knows how things would have gone for Jimmy and Ardis had not whispered rumor roused their marriage.

The Motorcycle

My office window is wide open. The slight breeze is strangely warm for early March, and strangely silent too. The birds aren't back yet. They could hardly know that it would be so warm so early. When I drove home from a pastoral visit yesterday afternoon, I saw that Oscar Cedergren was already out plowing one of his drier fields. He's early, but then Oscar just can't sit still for anything. He wouldn't dare plant yet. There's something intemperate and deceitful about 82 degrees on the eighth of March. It's like a promise that you know won't be kept or a gift that you know you'll have to give back.

Yet that first warmth, the smell of thawed earth, the sense of your own perspiration come again without effort, quickens something stilled by winter's necessary discipline. What quickened in me was memory of my 1961 Norton Single that rests in our garage underneath an old bedsheet. It was my only means of transportation for three years of college. Three springs I waited for the roads to clear and the weather to warm so that I could take the winter cover off. Not a spring has come since that the Norton has not crossed my mind.

It was hardly mere transportation, however. Riding a motorcycle had been for me a belated flirtation with adolescent recklessness and sensuousness. It was not just the speed that made the experience so alluring, but the directness with which the speed was experienced. The earth and the air flashed by at seventy miles an hour with nothing insulating me from concrete. The hot engine throbbed out power between my knees, the burst of thundering acceleration that came with a flick of the wrist. This motorcycle had also served as an eloquent statement of rebellion and independence from my parents, who had forbidden the purchase of a motorbike my junior year in high school.

It now lies surrounded by various paraphernalia of maturity: folded-up aluminum lawn chairs, a power mower, and Christopher's old playpen. I haven't ridden it in at least eight years. In fact, it doesn't run: the carburetor needs to be rebuilt, and both tires are shot. But I've never been able to let it go, even after it began to acquire antique value. Annie claims I hang on to it because it is emblematic of the youth I failed to misspend, but I have always—well, for eight years—planned to put it on the road again, which would probably make about the same statement to this little town that I was making to my mother twenty years ago. Actually, most everybody in town and certainly everybody at church knows about the Norton in the minister's garage. But it's one thing to own an old motorcycle that you used to ride when you were young; it's quite another to actually ride one when you're not quite so young and no longer indulged certain irresponsibilities.

Last fall, the motorcycle in my past led me to make an unusual pastoral visit. In November, I got a phone call at home from the front desk of Lutheran Hospital up in Mankato. The voice said that I had been asked for, by name, by one of the hospital's patients, a young woman from North Haven. Her name was Carmen Krepke and she had been in the hospital for over two months. There had been some sort of dreadful accident. I said I would stop in next week.

There are no Krepkes in Second Presbyterian. In fact I didn't know of anyone in North Haven with that name, so when I saw Angus at coffee hour on Sunday, I asked him if he knew a Carmen Krepke. He furrowed his brow and looked at me darkly. He said, "Hmmp, Carmen Krepke . . . sad story."

Carmen, he said, had spent most of her life doing her best to make her mother's life miserable. She was a sassy-pants at five; she was beating up boys when she was nine; she got kicked out of school in seventh grade for smoking cigarettes in the girls' room at the high school. Or maybe it was eighth grade, Angus allowed. Two years later she was skipping more school than she wasn't, and when she was seventeen, she got pregnant, dropped out of school, and married the father.

Angus was right. This was about the best any kid could do to make a parent's life miserable.

But there was more, Angus said. Two years later, she was tired of being married and tired of her now two-year-old, so she ran away with a motorcycle gang from Mankato called the Heathens. She left her baby with the husband, who moved home with his folks for a while, and then sensed a call to serve his nation and enlisted in the Navy. Angus told this story with an air of disgust, as if he were relating a cautionary tale of total depravity, a home-town illustration of how low young girls can sink once bad habits and ill discipline are given a toehold.

Now, Angus went on, Carmen was up in the hospital in Mankato in a body cast. She and one of the Heathens had crashed on a Harley-Davidson one Saturday night in September. He was killed outright. She had broken as many bones as the doctors could count, and had a concussion and some other problems inside. She nearly died, Angus said, implying that this would not have been an altogether unmerited fate.

He knew all this, he said, because Carmen's mother's sister cleans house for Minnie every other week. Elma, Carmen's mother, was visiting all the time with her daughter in the hospital, which rather surprised some people, what with all the kid had put her through. Elma, Angus said, was "real emotional," which was not so much a testimony to the depth of her feelings as critical comment about her inability to control them.

Control of feeling is a marker of virtue here. The family is Roman Catholic, Angus said in conclusion, "German R.C. Krepke's Elma's name, too, Carmen took it back after she deserted her husband and baby." I then told him about the phone call from the hospital and said I planned to call next Tuesday. This intrigued Angus. It intrigued me, too.

Carmen was in room 231, the orthopedic wing of the second floor of Lutheran. Two years earlier, they would have put her in pediatrics. The body cast was gone. One leg was in a cast up to her thigh and elevated with a pulley arrangement. Her hair was extremely short. I was sure most or all had been shaved off after the accident and was just coming back. She was very petite and fair. She was almost hard to see against the white linen of the hospital bed. Her appearance was most un-Carmenesque. I assumed the middle-aged woman sitting in a hard chair at the end of the bed to be Carmen's long-suffering mother, Elma. She was filling out the menu questionnaire for the next day.

I introduced myself. Carmen smiled and said, "Thanks for coming, Reverend, I'm Carmen, I've been born again. Do Presbyterians believe in visions?" I hadn't known what to expect, but this was not it. All the weight of this skeptical and psychologized culture of which I am a child put me on guard against such a claim, especially when made by a mixed-up young woman who had had a severe concussion and a recent brush with death.

She had loved Denny, she said. He was a Heathen, all right, but he had never hit her and was faithful to her. They were probably going to get married, she said. Tears came to her eyes. She missed him, she said, but was certain he was safe, because he wasn't really a heathen, not a "heathen Heathen." "That's just a name, you know, Reverend," she added for my edification.

"I was out of it for two weeks after the accident," Carmen said.

Her mother glanced up and explained: "She means she was unconscious, Reverend."

Then Carmen looked from her mother to me and whispered slowly and gravely: "When I woke up I had this picture in my head, I mean as clear as TV, just like TV in my head. And since then, Reverend, everything has looked different. I started reading out of the Bible that they put in the drawer of my nightstand." She showed me a red leatherette King James Version stamped "Gideons" on the bottom right corner of the cover. "And now everything has changed, I got born again." I glanced at her mother, who had that "all my prayers have been answered" look of immense relief.

Somehow, though, I had trouble feeling relieved. One part of me was almost ready to grasp her little white hand and say, "Praise the Lord, sister Carmen, praise the Lord, let us pray. . . ." Another part of me was considering the psychological impact of near-death on an emotionally immature young woman, the effects of a concussion and of all the painkillers that had been pumped into her little body. So I smiled weakly in what was surely a slightly patronizing manner and asked an obvious question in the style I had been taught in pastoral counseling classes: "You say you're living life with a new perspective?"

Carmen looked at me as if I were a none too bright child and said, "I asked you to come, because, you see, Mom's sister cleans for some people in your church and they said you got a bike and so I figured you'd understand about us and that we're not all a bunch of freaks and that Jesus could even love a no-good biker like me. I read in this Bible about this woman that Jesus met at a well who was a Samaritan or something, and everybody thought Samaritans were shit and He knew about all her divorces, but Jesus talked to her anyway and then she testified for Him. Do they let bikers in your church, Reverend?"

Carmen would not tell me about her vision. She had told no one, she said, not even her mother. But it was still with her, she said, "just like TV that never turns off," and because of it everything was different. We talked about her recovery and the hospital and the food and her doctors and then I offered to pray. Before I could speak my amen, Carmen was adding her own words: "Dear Jesus, I just thank you for savin' me from gettin' killed, and savin' me from gettin' sucked into darkness and for comin' to me in the hospital and lettin' me know that you were there.

And I pray for all the Heathens, too. Keep 'em outta trouble the best ya can. Amen."

I visited her about once a week for the next three months. I grew fond of her, although Elma I discovered to be less easy to love. She had led a victim's life and assumed the posture of those who believe the cosmos is in conspiracy against them. I came to respect Carmen for her candor and her valiant effort to love a difficult mother. But deeper even than this affection lay the strange appeal of Carmen's faith. To say that her faith was simply childlike would be unfair. Her experience with the Heathens and her brush with death lent authenticity and depth to her. Yet her faith did not examine itself. She saw no reason to second-guess experience, but just accepted it. She trusted her vision for what it seemed to her to be.

My life could never be portrayed in such a dramatic chiaroscuro of lights and darks. It has known no sudden turns, no conversions. My faith never stops looking at itself. It trusts nothing fully. It suspects every emotion to be mere sentiment. It scrutinizes every whispered intimation of divine presence as a possible deceit of the subconscious. I don't think I ever believed as Carmen does, not even when I was a child. I don't know that I can, or that I should.

The last time I saw her in the hospital was a Tuesday, a week ago tomorrow. She said the doctors were letting her out in two days and that she would be coming to church. I had heard such promises from hospital beds and knew that they were often forgotten later. I said I would look for her. Then she said she had something to give me.

Elma reached behind the nightstand and handed me a package. It was wrapped in brown and orange gift wrap and tied with orange ribbon. Inside was a painting done on black velvet. It showed a figure riding on a motorcycle away from the viewer and toward a white spot—a light, I supposed—set at a distance on the horizon. The rider had long dark hair and white robes swept back in the wind as the motorcycle sped toward the light. It was obviously Jesus—Jesus on a motorcycle. "It's a picture of my vision," Carmen said. "This occupational therapy lady from the hospital has been teaching me how to paint. I know he's not wearing a helmet—I suppose Jesus would have worn a helmet—but there was no helmet in my vision. It's a gift for the church. You can hang it in the entrance where people will see it right away when they come in."

That Sunday morning at ten-twenty, as I put on my pulpit robe to go pray with the choir before the service, I glanced out my office window and saw Elma and Carmen coming across the parking lot. Carmen was moving fast on her aluminum Canadian crutches. Elma strutted beside her as if this were her dancing day. I looked down at the black velvet painting of Jesus on the motorcycle leaning face to the wall behind my desk. "Annie," I said to my wife, who had stopped in to say hi before church, "quick, hang this picture on a wall someplace, anyplace."

After the service, Annie came through the greeting line and whispered to me, "Jesus on the Harley is hanging downstairs by the furnace room door." Twenty feet behind her were Carmen and Elma. Elma said indignantly that she had not noticed the painting in the entrance as they came in. She began to peer theatrically over my shoulder to the left and the right. The two of them waited as everybody else drifted off to the parlor for coffee. I escorted them downstairs to the boiler room door, where *Jesus on the Motorcycle* hung on the very nail that had held a Minnesota state boiler inspection certificate an hour earlier.

Carmen seemed pleased enough, but Elma was clearly not. How displeased I did not know until yesterday afternoon when I walked to the back of the church to find my hymnbook and noticed that *Jesus on the Motorcycle* was hanging prominently to the right of the sanctuary door. I shook my head and groaned. I lifted the painting off the wall and saw a neatly typed message taped to the plaster underneath. It read, "Do Not Remove This Picture. God Meant It To Be Here."

There was really only one thing to do. I called Carmen on the phone and told her that her painting was "extraordinary and altogether unique." (The truth.) Would it be asking too much if she were to give me permission to hang it on the wall of my office rather than in the church?

I'm looking at it right now. It is awful, I mean "awful" awful and "full of awe" awful. I don't know what I know about visions, but I do know that Carmen Krepke, who spent nineteen years of her life creating a hell, was in church this past Sunday. I know that she is suddenly much more patient with her mother than I could ever be. It's hard to believe that people change much, but sometimes they do. Grace does not necessarily move along the paths we know, the roads that are comfortable for us. Who knows with what strange vocabulary God may speak? Who knows what image the Divine may choose?

When Carmen said it would be okay for me to hang the picture in my office, she also told me that I "ought to get the Norton back on the road. It'd be good for ya to do some ridin'." I hung up the phone happily jostled again by Carmen's directness of speech and faith. She simply accepted experience as it came to her and for what it was. I guess that it is this trust in experience that so intrigues me. She trusted her love for Denny, the Heathen. She trusted Jesus, who came to her in a dream. She trusted the thrill of a motorcycle.

The weather turned cold last night: it's not supposed to get above thirty-five today and the TV was talking about freezing rain later. But I got up early this morning and went out to the garage and took the carburetor off the Norton. Jimmy Wilcox says he can rebuild it. And the weather will turn warm again.

Learning
to Dance

The Session met the Tuesday night before Palm Sunday. The five of our six elders present ambled into the Sunday school classroom at the end of the upstairs hall at about ten after eight. We always meet there because it has bigger chairs than the other rooms, but they're still not quite adult size. Everybody's knees stick up and we normally leave our coats on because it's cool, though not nearly as cold as the church parlor, where the only grown-up chairs are.

The only real item on the agenda was a matter referred to the Session by the Christian Education Committee. They had been asked by the advisors of the Westminster Fellowship, the church's youth group, that the "young people" be permitted to have a "sock hop" in the fellowship hall underneath the sanctuary. It was to be held the Friday after Easter. Nowhere but here has anything called a "sock hop" been held since about 1959, except as a sort of nostalgic indulgence in which the avant-garde of Minneapolis or Chicago demonstrate how avant they are by embracing as camp what is really very recent history.

At first, I thought that the Westminster Fellowship had chosen this name for their dance in order to clothe in fifties innocence a matter they knew would be contentious—namely dancing in church. But not so. Their choice of words was honest and without political intent. I discovered that their advisors, who remembered sock hops from their teenage years, had told them that dances held in church basements were called by this name.

The Session is normally supportive of youth activities. Because so many young families have left for the city, kids are an increasingly dear commodity in small towns. But even a sock hop, evoking as it does the innocent image of kids' feet in sweat socks on the old linoleum floor of the church basement, is still dancing, dancing in church. Never has there been dancing in Second Presbyterian Church, not even in the Fellowship Hall with its cinder block walls and well-stained suspended ceiling. Four and a half centuries of Calvinist inertia recoil at the idea of dancing anywhere in the house of the Lord.

"What kind of dancing would it be?" asked Arnie Peterson, who seemed cautiously open to this radical departure. "Well, you know," was the consensus answer, "the kind of dancin' kids do these days." But nobody had a clear picture in their head what kind of dancing that might be.

There followed a reflective silence in which the five Session members present appeared to be struggling to conjure up mental images of how sixteen-year-olds dance.

The quiet was broken by Angus MacDowell, who offered a bit of hard intelligence. He said that he had just been to visit his son and daughter-in-law in Spokane. "They get cable TV out there and one afternoon I was flippin' around with the remote control and on come something they call MTV. All the kids watch it, Larry told me. Well, I mean to tell ya, if this MTV is the kinda dancin' the kids are gonna do, we got trouble."

Angus's ensuing description of what he had witnessed on MTV was exhaustive, horrific, and persuasive: bizarre costumes, thunderous electric guitars, incomprehensible words, young people of indeterminate gender leaping and gyrating and making pained facial expressions into the camera. It occurred to me that Angus must have been tuned into MTV for a considerable time.

Arnie said that he doubted our kids would want to re-create such scenes in the Fellowship Hall, which everybody knew. But everybody still agreed that any kind of dancing was, well, dancing, and just didn't belong in the church. Inertia carried the day; the sock hop was voted down four to nothing with one abstention. The Session allowed that a well-supervised junior-senior high dance in one of the kids' basements, but not in the church, would be fine with them.

Over the next few days I found myself increasingly miffed by the inconsistency of the moral logic behind this thinking. Why should it be unacceptable for teenagers to dance in the church basement when it's fine for them to dance in their own basements? But it was more than ethical quirkiness that bothered me. Rather, it was the unspoken fear of outward, physical expression, the unspoken discomfort with movement, of letting feeling flow out into arms and legs, and underneath that, a fear of the body itself, especially, I suspected, a fear of young bodies. I brooded about it for the rest of the week, muttering to myself and my wife about hobbled spirits and the fear of spontaneity and joyless religion. By Thursday, we were joking about Elmer Gantry being right about "petrified Presbyterians."

Friday evening before Palm Sunday was Jimmy Wilcox's baby sister's wedding. I officiated, of course, standing in front of a row of eight nineteen- and twenty-year-olds, some of the girls so nervous that they had to bite their lips to keep the giggles at bay. All went well; it was a standard ceremony: Wagner at the beginning, Mendelssohn at the end, the soprano sang "The Wedding Song" and the uncle read 1 Corinthians 13.

Annie and I were invited to the reception, which was to be held at the Elks Club. We were late getting there, what with locking up the church and picking up the babysitter. The Elks Club is two miles outside of town on Highway 6. We approached with the car windows down to take in the evening air. From a good half mile away, we heard the "Beer Barrel Polka" reverberate across the soybean fields. Polka music was certainly not the couple's choice, but a largess granted by the bride's parents, who were, after all, paying the bills.

The inside of the Elks Club was hot, in spite of wide-open windows and doors. The place reeked of sweat and beer. Eddie Polanacheck and the Polka Aces, imported for the occasion from New Ulm, were onstage. Half the town was there, polka-ing up a storm, clapping their hands, drinking beer, and singing along with the wonderfully facile lyrics.

And right in the middle of the dance floor, kicking their legs back like hot polka dancers do, were the happy octogenarians, Angus and Minnie Mac-Dowell. They were smiling ear to ear and danced with little old steps, but in perfect time. Minnie's silver-gray hair, permed for the occasion, was bouncing in 2/4 time. When they saw me, they didn't stop dancing, they just stopped having fun doing it. They shifted to a sort of Presbyterian polka, that is, done decently and in order, with great attention to the details of process, but little outward enjoyment. Minnie's hair wasn't bouncing anymore. Angus stopped grinning and assumed an air of dutiful concentration meant to communicate that he was only dancing because Minnie wanted to.

When I sat down to write my Easter sermon that next week, I chose as my Old Testament text the story from II Samuel about King David danc-

ing before the Ark of the Covenant. This had
been no Hebrew sock hop, but an unrehearsed,
spontaneous dance of joy, done, so says Scripture,
in the raw, in the presence of God. The King of
Israel leaped about as the Law, tucked away its
box, was carried in procession to the Temple. David's princess wife watched all this and, like our
Session, disapproved of dancing in church, at least
without your clothes.

I titled the sermon "The Lord of the Dance." It
was Easter and the topic was resurrection, which I
said was God's dance of life. I referred to the story
of David's dance, but confess that I spiritualized
that narrative by disclaiming any notions that we
ought literally to imitate David. I speculated that
"in the heart of God there is a profound, vibrant,
dancing joy, and if there's a dancing joy in our
God, so there should be in us." I could not resist
ending the sermon with a few lines from the folk
hymn that lent me the sermon's title: "They cut
me down and I leap up high; I am the life that will
never, never die. . . . Dance then, wherever you
may be; I am the Lord of the Dance said He, And
I'll lead you all, wherever you may be, And I'll
lead you all in the dance said He."

In the prayers after the sermon, I dared to pray
"that we, Your people, might be filled with Your
joy, that our hearts might dance as David danced
before the Ark, that we might dance for the good-
ness of life." During silent prayer, I asked that
God might deepen in me the joy of faith, touch

me often with the joy of laughter, and fill me with the spirit of dance.

They say that you should be careful about what you pray for, because you're liable to get it. I hardly dreamed that my prayer would be answered so soon. I said, "Amen," and "let us now receive the offering." I sat down, the four ushers soberly passed the plates while the organist played a somber and tuneless little ditty. When the offering had been collected, she modulated jerkily into the Doxology, and the ushers marched down the aisle, wooden plates in their hands.

They stopped at the foot of the five carpeted steps that lead up to our very elevated chancel where the communion table sits and where the offering plates are to be placed when full. I always offer a Prayer of Dedication from the top of the steps and, because it's too far to reach, then walk down to get the plates.

All went as usual until I turned, a plate in each hand, to mount the steps to the chancel and place the offering on the communion table. The hem of my robe had come loose and as I took the first step, my toe caught it. But I didn't fall. I should have backed down then and there, but years of liturgical habit kept me aimed onward and upward. With my next step, I was further inside the garment. By the time I was to the third step, I realized that I was walking up the inside of my black Geneva pulpit robe. I was nearly on my knees; I could have turned around and sat down on the steps, freed my feet, and started over. It would have been a small indignity, but it is what I should have done.

But I decided to stay the course. I straightened up with all my might. My robe gave way and ripped right at the bottom button. The force of this sudden freedom sent my arms jerking upward. I managed to hold on to the offering plates, but all their contents flew up and back over my head. Offering envelopes, dollar bills, five-dollar bills, quarters, dimes, and nickels rained down upon the heads of four stunned ushers.

Well, my feet were free, but pride still bound my will. I should have turned around to the congregation, bowed theatrically, and accepted the humorous and humbling grace of the moment. But I marched on up the steps as though nothing had happened, and laid the four empty offering plates on the table. The ushers marched back down the aisle through all the offertory debris.

I turned around to return to the pulpit and dared a glance at the larger than usual Easter Sunday congregation. What I saw were the tops of one hundred twenty heads, bowed deeply in prayer so they would not have to look at me. There was not a hint of hilarity, not a giggle or a titter, although I believe that I saw the silk flowers on Ardis Wilcox's Easter bonnet shaking as though she were stifling laughter. We sang the closing hymn without looking at each other. Angus MacDowell and Jimmy Wilcox used the hymn as cover to deftly gather up the offering scattered over the front third of the church. As I stood in the greeting line after the sermon, two elderly ladies offered to repair my robe and Arnie Peterson asked with a wink if I'd had a nice trip. Then he slapped me on the arm and said, "Well, see ya next fall." That stale joke was the nearest anybody came, myself included, to laughing aloud at the accidental offertory dance before the altar of God.

In the sermon I had soberly pronounced that "in the heart of God there is a profound, vibrant, dancing joy." I had prayed, "Lord, teach me to dance." Perhaps that prayer was answered and I was presented with a first dancing lesson. To dance, I guess you must be willing to play the fool a bit. In some eyes, all dancing, gratuitous movement that it is, will look foolish. To dance, you must step away from that burdensome consciousness of self. Faith is a dance with divinity, a mad polka done on the grave, kicking your legs back, and shouting out polka "whoops" like the fool you are. And maybe we should even throw money in the air. We should certainly laugh at ourselves when we trip.

I guess that I had not really heard my own Easter sermon. Insecurity stiffened my pride, and I dared not dance when I was asked. Perhaps I will be able to when invited next time.

A Strange Providence

We have weathered another Easter. It always leaves me tired and full of hope—the same kind of tired and full of hope that comes after a long spring day in your vegetable garden. Hard work, no tomatoes yet, but good reason for hope. The Easter Sunday service was packed with the usual holiday contingent of visiting relatives—mostly children and grandchildren come back from assorted suburbs of Minneapolis and Chicago to what some still call home. Then there were a number of locals who surface in church twice a year, drawn up from the murky depths of backsliding by some ancestral memory of poinsettias or lilies and perhaps faith.

Annie and I took a few days off the week after Easter and went up to the Cities. We stayed two nights at the Radisson, saw *Cats,* and ate in a Northern Italian restaurant we couldn't afford. Like most tourists, we did our very best not to look like tourists. You do this by walking very fast and being careful not to look up at the IDS Tower or say "excuse me" to people you bump into. You also have to pretend that you're quite accustomed to paying $21.95 for Veal Marsala that doesn't include the salad, and that you're used to seeing people sleeping on the sidewalk and relieving themselves from a curb.

But the hardest part of pretending not to be a tourist from the sticks is resisting the sore temptation to say hi to people you really don't know, in those careless words revealing the painful truth that you come from somewhere small and in two days you'll be sent back to where you belong. We had the same waiter three times at the restaurant at the Radisson, twice for breakfast and once for lunch. He was sternly efficient and said "eggs Sardou" as if he maybe could speak French. But his name tag said he was "Andrew."

The second time he waited on us, it was all we could do to resist the habit of four years in a small town and say: "Well, Andy, good morning, good morning, how about this! How are ya today? Doesn't seem quite so busy as yesterday, does it?" Instead, I offered a crisp "good morning," and asked for two coffees. No way he could guess from that we were anything but a couple of sophisticates catching a bite before heading for our offices.

We drove home Thursday afternoon. It had been ages since either of us had been anywhere more exotic than Mankato. Four years had passed since I took the call to go to North Haven. In our minds, it had always been a first solo pastorate, a place to get a start on a mercurial career in the ministry, a place to pass through. Pastors of Second Presbyterian have seldom stayed longer than three or four years.

So it was strange to feel, as we have these last months, that ours was one road show that might stay in town for a while. Driving home on Highway 169 that afternoon, we found a common intuition becoming words. There was a rightness about us in that little town: Annie comfortable, the kids barely remembering anywhere else, and my work at church accepted, sometimes indulged, but always graciously received. So we said what had been hanging in our thoughts: "Let's go home and think of it as home, and make it home for a while." For the first time in my four years in North Haven, I felt I understood what it meant to be called to be a pastor someplace.

We stopped and picked up the kids at the sitter's and went home to find a note tucked in the screen door. It was from Maureen, our eight-hour-a-week volunteer church secretary. It read: "Minnie MacDowell is pretty sick, thinks she's dying again, better get over there when you get back." Minnie is eighty-six and married to Angus. For the last ten years, she has been very organized about dying. She plans to do it "just so" because she has always done everything "just so." This means she'll do it at home, in bed, with a fresh nightgown on and the pastor present. There have been two false alarms in the last three years. As the doctor explained to me: "The only problem with Minnie's plans is that she's not sick."

So I climbed right back in the car and headed over to the MacDowells'. Angus greeted me at the door with a grave look, but then Angus has had a grave look since he was twenty-two, or so they tell me. "Thanks for coming, David." He put his hand on my back just below my neck and gently shepherded me toward the staircase of their old Victorian house. Minnie was upstairs in bed, in a lacy nightgown, her hair newly done, the bedcovers neatly folded just above her waist. She languidly raised her arm for me to take her hand, smiled theatrically, and said, "I'm so glad you made it back in time, Pastor."

Angus pushed a chair at me from the rear. I sat down, let a moment pass, and asked Minnie if she were comfortable. She nodded slowly and said that the doctor had just left but had been no help. I was getting up nerve to inquire about what the doctor had said, when Minnie, perhaps sensing what I was thinking, said, "Ask me the question, Pastor."

The question, I had come to know on my last two visits to Minnie's deathbed, was an essential part of her very precise plans for the day. It was a question that she had been raised to believe was absolutely necessary for a tasteful death. The pastor was to ask: "Are you prepared to die?" The die-ee was to answer: "Yes, Pastor, I am." Then the pastor read the Twenty-third Psalm and prayed briefly, concluding with the Lord's Prayer.

Then the die-ee died. That was how it was properly done. We had done it twice before, all except for the last part.

I looked helplessly over my shoulder at Angus, who knit his brow and nodded imperceptibly, which I took to mean "Do your job, kid." So I smiled pastorally at Minnie and said, "Are you prepared to die?"

I almost slid off my chair when she said, "No." Her lower lip started to quiver and she looked away from me at the wall.

I squeezed her hand as Angus patted me on the back and said, "Minnie's got something she's got to get off her chest."

At which Minnie choked out the words: "No, Angus, you tell him."

"David," Angus began, "you'll remember that I was the chairman of the Pulpit Nominating Committee that called you to be our pastor four years ago." I remembered. It had been a committee of only three. They had been through the pastor search process so often as to wink at some of the rules and not take the whole matter with the customary gravity. But as Angus began the tale, he was grave, even for Angus.

"We received twenty-eight dossiers from ministers. We read them all and narrowed the choice down to two, you and the Reverend Mr. Hartwick Benson of Indianapolis. We invited both you and Mr. Benson to visit North Haven. We listened to the both of you preach up in Willmar."

It came back to me as though it were yesterday:

a hot day in June, a brand-new pulpit robe fresh from Bentley and Simon, my champion fits-all sermon, my voice cracking during what was meant to be a thunderous conclusion. After it was over, I made my peace with the prospect of settling for a position even less desirable than North Haven, Minnesota. What elation, what affirmation, when a simple handwritten note came four days later postmarked "N. Haven, Minn." There was no heading, only a date, and then "Dear Sir: We are most pleased to inform you . . ."

"David," Angus went on as his eyes shifted from me to his wife, "Minnie was secretary to our committee. She typed up all the letters. She typed up one to Reverend Benson and one to you. Somehow they got into the wrong envelopes. Mr. Benson got your letter and you got Mr. Benson's letter."

At this, Minnie started dabbing her eyes with her hanky and then wrapping it tightly around her index finger in a sort of penitential self-mortification. "We never realized the mistake until you called on the phone to say yes, you'd come. You were so eager, we just decided, well, what the heck, and let it go. A few weeks later, I heard Mr. Hartwick Benson got a call to a church in Hawaii." Angus put his hand on my shoulder and gave a squeeze (a gush of empathy for Angus). Minnie was slowly shaking her head. She said, "I just couldn't die with such a thing on my conscience."

But all of a sudden, it wasn't Minnie who was

dying, it was me. Noting my stunned silence, she pushed herself up to a sitting position, ordered Angus to make hot tea, and resolved to postpone her death. They served me tea with shortbread, and Angus commented how amazingly helpful my visit was to the state of Minnie's health. Looking sideways at her, he said to me, "A person always feels better when they get something off their chest." Their souls may have been unburdened, but mine was loaded. I got in the car and headed home, wherever that was.

This near-deathbed revelation derailed the sense of rightness about being in North Haven that Annie and I had felt just a few hours ago. That wave of acceptance that had washed over us as we drove home was receding to the sea. My "call" was nothing but Minnie mixing up two letters.

I drove north on Main toward the bridge and pulled over to the side of the road on the northeast edge of town. The slough that lies alongside the road is an elbow-shaped marsh that used to be a bend in the river until the river changed course some eighty years ago. North Haven, built on the river, suddenly found itself a half mile away, astride a languid stretch of shallow water and marshland that went nowhere. "Stranded water, the river not where it was supposed to be," I said to myself. It was very quiet. I heard a blue heron call and then saw it take to wing. There are no herons on the river itself. The water moves too fast and there are too many boats. There was a rightness about this marsh that should have been the river. The heron, the cattails, the evening breeze just troubling the shallow water. It wasn't supposed to be this way, but it was.

A memory came to me from my seminary days. A strident old Calvinist professor of theology was lecturing on the will of God. He had argued hard for a high view of providence. To make the point perfectly clear, he ambled over to the classroom window and said, "Do you see that man leaning on that lamppost by the bus stop down there?" I could see him then and I can see him in my mind's eye now. He was wearing a business suit and a hat and was fumbling in his pocket for something. After we had all had a look, the professor paused dramatically, and said slowly, "From the very beginning of time, God has intended that man to be standing there at this very moment."

We didn't like the idea. It rankled all our notions of free will and human independence. I remember some pundit in the class asking, "But what if he just got off at the wrong bus stop?"

The professor raised his eyebrows and replied, "The wrong bus stop from whose point of view?"

I know that so much that has come upon me in life I did not search out and choose, but rather found by chance and accepted as grace. The will of God is an infinitely intricate weaving of incidents and accidents, plans and providence. Sometimes it works through us, sometimes in spite of us, but in all things, it can work for good. The rightness Annie and I had felt about North Haven that afternoon was not diminished by a decision made four years ago to call Hartwick Benson as pastor. It was probably a good choice. He was older and more experienced than I.

This is home because Minnie and a few hundred other people trust me to hold their hands should they die. It is home because Angus and Minnie dared to tell me the truth. It is home because old ladies reach out to touch our children as they pass by in church as if they were their own. It is home because the checker in the market calls me by my name. It is home because I don't want to go anywhere else. What I know now is that how this came to be home is a stranger story than I had thought. But the story usually is stranger than we first thought. I drove home to tell Annie that Minnie MacDowell had lived to die another day and that I thought I knew where home was.

Reunion

This past week Annie and I made it back to my old hometown, Peeksborough, Pennsylvania. Our trip was fairly big news here in North Haven, making lead story in the *North Haven Herald*'s "Out and About" column. Other people's business, especially their travels, dinner guests, and hospitalizations, constitute hard news in a town like this. When Angus and Minnie took their big trip to England and Scotland two years ago, the *Herald* did a four-week series with pictures.

Our trip to Peeksborough was occasioned by an invitation I got in the mail back in March to attend my high school class reunion. "The Class of '68, Peeksborough High School, cordially invites YOU to Attend a Reunion Gala." Enclosed was a schedule listing precisely what constitutes a "gala" in suburban Philadelphia, all of which sounded singularly tame, even by the standards we've become accustomed to here. Also enclosed was a listing of the eighty-three members of the class of '68, where they were living and what they were doing, more or less.

I scanned the list and immediately decided that I would not be going. Under the address column, I saw places like San Jose, Dallas, Chicago, and Stamford, Connecticut. And then there was me: "Battles, Rev. David, Northaven, Minnesota." They didn't even get the place spelled right.

I imagined my classmates reading the list, seeing my address, and thinking to themselves, *Northaven. Northaven. I wonder if that's one of those tony suburbs west of the Twin Cities.* Then I imagined them getting out their Rand McNally Road Atlases and looking up Northaven to see just where I'd ended up. First they'd see that the reunion committee had spelled it wrong. It would say, "North Haven, pop. 1,820, F-4." Then they would think to themselves, *Whoa! Eighteen hundred people—EXCLUSIVE suburban enclave.* Then they'd look back on page 43-4 of the atlas, find the little "F" and the little "4," and discover that the "F" and "4" intersect somewhere in the middle of nowhere to the west of Mankato. Big grins would wash over their faces, and they would make little "hmm, hmm, hmm" noises and maybe mumble something like "Well, well, well, how about Davy Battles preaching to the farmers out in the sticks."

"I'm not going to go," I told Annie, "no way. They're all going to ask, 'When did you decide to enter the ministry, Dave?' And they're going to expect some sort of Peter Marshall answer about almost falling over a cliff in the fog. Then they're going to talk about the arts in southwestern Con-

necticut and the housing prices in Chicago. I can't
do it, Annie. I won't go."

The theory is that class reunions are guileless
celebrations of the halcyon days of high school.
But I knew better; in fact, everybody knows better. High school reunions are inspections, exami-
nations, tests. Everybody sees what everybody else
has or has not made of themselves. It's all closely
graded and clearly understood but unspoken: attractiveness of wives/handsomeness of husbands,
cleverness of children, weight gained/hair lost,
address/size of home, the potent/impotent ring
of your job title. This reunion was a midterm.
Everybody was forty or so—halfway through the
Big Term. "No," I said, "I won't go."

It was Annie who changed my mind. She said
she would go with me and would never leave my
side. And she pointed out that I would be graded
high in the "attractiveness of wife" area. She also
noted that one third of the class of '68 had never
left Peeksborough and then she made her power
play: "Dave, wouldn't it be great to see Darleen
MacClean again? I see she's on the reunion committee."

In high school, Darleen and I had been a four-
year item. All through high school we "went
steady," as it was put then. We got pinned in our
senior year and she wore my class ring on a chain
around her neck. Locally, Darleen had been con-
sidered quite a catch: oval-faced, blue-eyed, and
full-figured. She was no student, but a shoe-in for
homecoming queen. In the eyes of the world, or

at least in the eyes of my male classmates, keeping my hands on Darleen for four years may well have been my greatest conspicuous achievement.

Our relationship was revealed for what it was in my freshman year of college. After about three months apart, I realized I neither liked nor disliked Darleen MacClean; the fact was, I didn't know her. What I had liked was local notoriety and social stability.

But she was not forgotten. Annie had never met Darleen, who had with the years metamorphosed in my wife's mind into a sort of eastern Pennsylvania Bo Derek. In the course of our marriage, I have fallen into the perverse habit of negotiating Darleen into conversations with my wife at strategic moments. I do this half consciously, half deliberately, a little teasingly. When I say "Darleen MacClean, the Homecoming Queen," it always carries the same unspoken message: "Dear wife, I once dated a beauty queen, but I chose you."

We walked into the old high school in Peeksborough and my first impression was the familiar smell of the floor wax. It carried me back twenty years. They say that of the five senses, smell and taste remain in memory the best. Annie and I walked together down the long hall toward the gym. It was like a tunnel through time conjuring up not so much specific memories of events or people, but the vaguer memories of emotions, especially the insecurity and anxiety of adolescence. Above the door of the gymnasium was a big sign

—poster paint on white butcher paper—reading "Welcome, Class of '68!" Underneath the sign was Darleen MacClean sitting next to a card table labeled "Registration."

The years had not been kind. Her hairstyle, a beehive, had not changed. But round-faced and full-figured had become just round and full. She was wearing too much makeup and a dress too young for her years, inappropriate to her age, and too tight for her shape. The effect was not Bo Derek. She and I squealed our greetings, embraced, and I said, "This is Annie, my wife."

Annie, God bless her gracious soul, greeted Darleen like a peasant presented to royalty. "I've heard so much about you from David. What a pleasure it is to finally meet you in person." We exchanged smiles and nostalgic sighs and the names and ages of our kids. Then we registered and moved toward the gym. I didn't even dare look at Annie. I expected at least a playful look or an elbow in my ribs, or maybe, at worst, a "Darleen, the Homecoming Queen." But I got nothing, not a word from her, and it's been over a week now.

The reunion committee had chosen the South Seas as the theme, Polynesia as Pennsylvania imagines it to be. We meandered over to a table on which were set two huge punch bowls. One was labeled "Bali-High Punch (alcoholic)," and the other "Bali-High Punch (nonalcoholic)." Gathered there, with clear plastic glasses filled with one or the other variation, were two former classmates. I remembered both of them right off, though I'd thought of neither for twenty years.

John ("call me Jack") Arnold had been voted "most likely to succeed" by the class of '68. Jack was born smooth, one of those souls who slide through life with everything moving into place or out of their way. He had been popular, a jock who had graduated near the top of the class. He had gone to Temple on scholarship and ended up, I'd heard, with an M.B.A.

The other person at the Bali-High Punch table was Andy Starrett, who graduated as one of the eighty-three members of our class but whom almost nobody seemed to know. He grew up in a neighborhood of mobile homes on the edge of town. His family kept to themselves. His mother did cleaning work and his father drank. Andy was quiet and eclectically bookish—I remembered him always reading sci-fi paperbacks. He never missed school and always missed extracurricular activities.

But he didn't miss the senior prom. Against his better judgment, somebody had bamboozled him into a double date. I can still see him: white rent-a-tux, Beatles haircut, and a lost, overawed look on his face. The theme had been Polynesia that time as well. Halfway through the evening, Andy's old man burst into the decorated gym filthy drunk and yelling his head off about "the car." He knocked over a papier-mâché palm tree and dragged his son out into the parking lot, where he beat him silly, probably because he was young and had a tux on.

There could not have been a more unlikely pair in conversation at the Bali-High Punch table than these two. Jack was showing Andy pictures of his lovely kids and lovely second wife. At least the kids and the second wife were in the foreground of all the pictures. But the photos were really pictures of the backgrounds: there was the wife in front of the Mercedes, with just enough of the front fender revealed so that you knew what it was. There was a snowy shot of the kids in ski jackets squinting at the camera in front of the five-bedroom colonial in Short Hills. There was the whole family on a rustic front porch—"the place up in Maine." Finally, there were the kids in lifejackets on the boat.

After the pictures were over, Jack talked about his mortgage insurance business in the Cleveland suburbs. Andy asked an appropriate question about softness in the real estate market and then about how his company handled foreclosures. Jack rambled on about "the S-and-L thing" and ended the conversation tapping Andy's lapel with the index finger of the same hand that was holding his half-filled plastic glass. A little Bali-High Punch sloshed on Andy's jacket. "You know what keeps me on top," he was saying, "know-how, know-how keeps me on top. Tell me, what are you up to?" Andy got two sentences out before Jack's eye caught sight of another subject. "Jimmy, ol' buddy!" he called out, raising his drink in the air. Over his shoulder he said, "Good to talk," and was off. We watched him hustle over to Jimmy.

Out came the pictures and I caught the words, "growing mortgage insurance firm . . ."

I looked at Andy. He looked at me and smiled. I said, "I really would like to know what you're doing." He had gone to a state school and majored in psychology. He specialized in alcohol treatment and now was the director of a small treatment facility in Pittsburgh. He saw a few successes, he said, and he and his teenage sons did a lot of bicycling together. He liked to read and had written a science fiction novel that he couldn't get published. He smiled and raised his glass of Bali-High Punch and said, "Good life, how about you?"

He listened to me, nodding and smiling like a seasoned counselor. He asked questions that showed he heard what I had said. We talked for a good forty minutes, me and the kid nobody noticed. His wife came by and slipped an arm around his waist. Jack was across the gym and still dealing his photos to all who would give him a chance. We caught each other's eyes and Andy said, with more mischief than guile: "He reminds me of a story, the old chestnut about the two Indian gurus sitting in front of their cave meditating. A jetliner flies over and the one guru says, 'They have the know-how.' And the other one answers, 'Yes, but do they have the know-why?' "

The drive home took two days. Mile after mile of Pennsylvania, Ohio, Indiana, and Wisconsin slipped by, giving me time to think. What I thought was that I was glad Annie talked me into the trip. I thought of the kid nobody had ever noticed and the kid everybody had always noticed and how their lives had taken shape. Maybe Jack had just grown into our expectations of him. He was indeed "most likely to succeed," and I suppose everybody at the reunion thought him a success, even if they were dodging him and his pictures by eleven. Nobody had had any expectations for Andy Starrett to grow into, so I guess he made up his own.

A few weeks later, it fell to me to preach the baccalaureate sermon to the seniors of North Haven High. It's one of those clergy jobs that, in a small town, gets rotated among the pastors each year. I preached briefly (although I'm sure they didn't think so) on a passage from Romans: "Do not be conformed to this world, but be transformed by the renewal of your mind." I looked at these babies, all lined up in rows, sweating miserably in their rented acrylic robes, mortarboards perched unnaturally on their heads. Who would they be in twenty years? How would they come back to their reunion in the year 2010? Would they be conformed—and if so, conformed to what? Would they be transformed—and if so, transformed by what power? Only time will tell, time and grace.

Lamont Wilcox's Boat

There really is no such thing as privacy in a town like this. As in all the villages that ever were, people pretty much know and have always known each other's business. Current notions of privacy and anonymity are urban luxuries. The anonymity of city apartment blocks and the privacy of detached suburban ranch homes do offer a certain liberation. They also offer danger. Since the dawn of time, the question "But what will people think?" has put a fence around even vaguely aberrant behavior. If nobody knows or cares, the fence is gone. Terrible things can happen. Wonderful things, too.

People who want to be different, or simply *are* different, have three choices in a place like this. First, they can leave. A lot of them do, which is why places like Mankato and New York City are full of strange and creative people. These people mostly came from someplace else, often someplace small, where life would have been uphill had they stayed.

The second choice for people who are different is to stay and try to be extraordinarily discreet. This seldom works for long. The third alternative for different people is to stay and become a local character. Every town has a few. Often, such local characters are, in time, not just tolerated, but veritably celebrated with the knowing smiles of a resigned acceptance. A lot of small towns even take a certain pride in their characters. But they are talked about. To stay is a brave choice.

Larry Wilcox's older brother, Lamont, chose to stay. That is, he chose to stay until three years ago last spring. Lamont left town when he was forty-eight. His manner of leaving was the most dramatic exit anybody in North Haven remembers. (Second place in dramatic exits is usually assigned to my predecessor, the Reverend Mr. Paulsen, whose story I have already told you.)

People talked about Lamont on a number of counts. Most conspicuously, he didn't work. More precisely, he didn't work at anything that earned money to support himself and his family. He had inherited the farm, such as it was, leased out the tillable acreage, and lived in the farmhouse. The white paint has been peeling off the house for as long as anybody can remember. Bales of hay are stacked around the foundation to keep the cold out.

People also talked about Lamont because "he drank." In local parlance, "to drink" means to drink to excess and implies alcoholism. This was clearly the case with Lamont, who "drank" since he was in high school. There are any number of private alcoholics in town, but Lamont was thoroughly public in his insobriety. All his drinking was done at the Blue Spruce Bar and Grille. But he only drank in the evening, which began about three-thirty.

What people mostly talked about, however, was the boat Lamont was building in the barn next to the farmhouse. He had started work on the boat in the summer of 1959 after finishing the last of C. S. Forester's Horatio Hornblower novels. The first of that series of hearty nautical adventures had been assigned by the late Miss Pratt to her Junior English Lit. class at North Haven High. Later, she often confessed that she regretted having ever exposed young Lamont to such fancies. It would have been better, she said, to have assigned Lamont Ole Rölvaag's *Giants in the Earth*. But the sea had captured Lamont. He closed the last page of the Hornblower series and announced to his mother that he was going to build a boat in the barn, and that when the boat was finished, he was going to sail to the Caribbean.

People talked about "the boat" because Lamont kept feeding the town conversational material. At the Blue Spruce, he would announce something like "I got that starboard chain plate bolted to the bulkhead this morning." Such an announcement might as well have been made in Swahili. It required translation, which Lamont was pleased to offer over "a few beers," and technical diagrams, which he drew on bar napkins. This kept "the boat" a lively topic of gossip and, of course, scorn. Critics noted that Lamont had never even seen the ocean. To this he would reply, "That's why I'm building a boat." Others noted that thirty years was a long time to be working on a single vessel, whatever the size. To this Lamont would answer, "A vessel to sail open waters needs to be well and fully founded." True, of course, but Lamont's workdays started late and ended early.

But most every conversation about Lamont's boat concluded with an almost liturgical repetition of two points, both ancient and true. First, the nearest navigable water to Lamont's barn was a good 140 miles away at Lake Pepin on the Mississippi River. Second, nobody in town had ever seen "the boat." Lamont kept the barn locked and refused to show anybody his project. He said they would only see it when it was done. Nobody was foolish enough to think that this day would ever come. Some radical skeptics doubted the very existence of "the boat."

Lamont's wife, Annette, is a teller in the Farmer's and Merchant's Bank. She always talked freely about Lamont's foolishness and made it clear that she had no interest at all in boats. Both the kids are grown and gone to Minneapolis. To say that Annette was pitied would not be quite accurate. She bore the burden of Lamont Wilcox as a martyr wears a crown. She often picked him up at the Blue Spruce when it was too cold to walk home.

"Drunks can freeze to death in the winter," she would say. She alternatively defended and scolded him in public. Over twenty-five years of marriage, a certain symbiosis had developed between the drunken dreamer and the stalwart wife. Both seemed comfortable with their roles. If one of Annette's friends said over coffee, "Annette, I just don't know how you put up with it," Annette would lift her chin, purse her lips, and nod ever so slightly. "A woman of steel, I am" those movements said, "a giant of the earth."

If Annette was surprised when Lamont announced that "the boat" was finished and that he would be leaving at the end of June, she didn't show it. Stoicism was her adopted style. The town, however, could speak of nothing else. It was as though we were about to hear the punch line of a joke that had been three decades in the telling.

Bud Jennerson made "the boat" the lead story in that week's issue of the *Herald:* LOCAL MAN TO EMBARK ON SOLO VOYAGE ABOARD HOME-MADE VESSEL. The "home-made vessel" was, Bud reported, a twenty-nine–foot sailboat made of plywood and fiberglass "from plans purchased by Mr. Wilcox from the Glen-L Marine Company of Tonawanda, New York, in 1959." She was named *Lady Barbara* (after the second wife of Horatio Hornblower). The story concluded: "On Thursday, the 21st of June, a flatbed tractor trailer from the Sorensen Trucking Corp. in Mankato will haul the *Lady Barbara* to Winona where she will be launched in the Mississippi River. From thence Mr. Wilcox will begin a voyage down that River to the Gulf of Mexico, then on to Florida, and finally to the Caribbean Islands."

Thursday, the twenty-first of June, is a day that will live long in the town's memory. By nine o'clock, the Wilcox driveway and the road in front of their place was lined with parked cars. The tractor part of the flatbed tractor trailer from Sorensen Trucking was protruding from the Wilcox's unpainted barn. The trailer part, onto which the *Lady Barbara* had been moved the night before by a system of jacks, was hidden in the barn's darkness. At about ten o'clock, the driver climbed into the cab, started the engine, and began to inch forward. The *Lady Barbara* emerged into the morning light to the cheers of former skeptics.

Lamont was standing in her cockpit, one hand on the tiller and the other waving to the crowd with the figure-8 wave of a beauty queen on the trunk of a convertible. On his head was a dark blue captain's hat with gold embroidery on the brim. Annette was standing by the kitchen door with her arms folded in front of her.

Lamont wrote a series of articles from aboard the *Lady Barbara* as she progressed on her journeys. Bud published every one of them in the *Herald*. They were travelogue in content and as close in style to C. S. Forester as Lamont could manage. The articles chronicled his voyage down the Mississippi and a three-month wait in New Orleans for the hurricane season to be over. A rigging failure in the Gulf of Mexico was described in detail, along with descriptions of the dangers such an accident might present in shark-infested waters. Next came Florida, where some unchronicled months passed before the *Lady Barbara* embarked for the Caribbean. Thereafter the articles became less regular and the voyage more difficult to follow. After ten months, the saga of the *Lady Barbara* ended in a harbor on an island off the coast of Venezuela when a seacock failed and she sank in waters too deep to permit salvage.

Lamont didn't come straight home. Perhaps he couldn't face the town after such an inglorious climax to his voyage. Maybe he couldn't face home without the dream of being somewhere else. Maybe he just didn't have the money for the airfare. Whatever, Lamont got a job on an oil rig off the coast of Venezuela and two months later took another oil rig job in the North Slope oil fields in Alaska, where he spent the last two winters.

He wrote Annette with regularity and she frequently dropped references around town to "when Lamont gets back." She remained "Mrs. Lamont Wilcox" and seemed no more daunted by his absence than if he had gone to Minneapolis to buy brass screws and fiberglass resin. The eventuality of his return was widely disputed. But, of course, Lamont Wilcox had surprised the town once before.

Lamont came home three months ago on a bright February day. He had written Annette that he was coming and that he had a present for her. The present was a new silver-gray Chevy Caprice. The North Slope oil fields pay well. Lamont looked fabulous. He had lost weight laboring on the oil rigs—even his beer belly was gone. In fact, Lamont announced to an incredulous town and even more incredulous wife that he no longer drank.

A sober Lamont who no longer lived spiritually in the Caribbean was a new creation altogether. He moved home, painted the house and the barn, got a part-time job in the feed and grain, and announced that he would cancel the leases and till his own acreage this season. In less than two months, Annette filed for divorce.

Lamont came to see me. I was officially his pastor, though I knew of him more than I knew him. He had been away most of my years in North Haven. He had that "I've been to hell and back" demeanor of most recovering alcoholics. But he had learned the wisdom of the broken and took Annette's decision to divorce him with resignation. "They warned me in A.A. that this might happen," he explained. The North Slope, he explained, had its own Alcoholics Anonymous chapter.

I said I just didn't understand. "For twenty-five years of your marriage you ended every day drunk and for the last three you've been gone. Through all of this Annette was faithful and patient. Now you come home sober and ready to work and she's

off to the lawyer. It just doesn't make sense, Lamont."

Lamont looked down and rubbed his forehead
with his thumb and index finger. Then he looked
at me and said, "Let me tell you a story, Dave. I
heard it from this guy who lived for years in
Kotzebue on the Bering Sea up in Alaska. He
worked for the National Wildlife Refuge. It's a
remote spot, Kotzebue, even for Alaska. Used to
be the supply ships came in only once a year. I
mean, all your food for the whole year except for
game came in on one boat: canned goods, flour,
sugar, some vegetables, even eggs.

"My friend and his wife liked their eggs for
breakfast. This was before they discovered choles-
terol. They would order a whole year's supply.
Eggs keep if you refrigerate them, which is no
problem in Kotzebue. I mean, they don't go rot-
ten, but they, well, change. Every morning my
friend and his wife would have their eggs, over
easy, sunny-side up, scrambled. They tasted fine.
Didn't really notice any change one day to the
next as the months went by. Finally, they were
eating year-old eggs, waiting for the boat to come
in with fresh. Then the boat would come in and
bring eggs that weren't a year old and my friend
and his wife would fry them up—and those fresh
eggs would taste just awful. He said they would
want to spit them out the first few days. They
would look for some of the old ones to fix. You
see, they got so accustomed to stale eggs that they
liked them better than the fresh. In fact, after a

year of stale eggs, they could hardly abide the real thing."

Lamont leaned back in his chair, smiled, and raised his eyebrows. "For twenty years Annette lived her life around Lamont the drunken dreamer. She's a good woman, Reverend, a hell-uva woman. She got used to living that way. I think she even kind of liked it. Patching up for me, apologizing for me, bitching about me, that was how she lived her life. She played sober and I played drunk. I was lost in a dream; she lived in reality. I was weak; she was strong. When I came home sober, it was like fresh eggs after twenty years of stale. And she couldn't stand the taste. People are like that, Reverend. They get used to the stale and prefer it to the fresh. They get used to the fake and like it better than the real thing."

As it turned out, a sober Lamont was at a loss to figure out where he fit into North Haven. So he moved to Minneapolis, where he has success-fully introduced himself to his children and grand-child. Larry told me he got a job selling boats at a marina in Wayzata.

I talked to Annette while she was working in the bank the other day. As she counted out three tens and four fives for me she said, "Lamont said he went to see you before he left." It was more a question than a statement. I put the money in my wallet and said, "Ya, he just needed to talk." She looked away from me. Her eyes began to moisten. She bit her lower lip but not a tear rolled down her cheek. "Twenty years I put up with his drinking. Let me tell you, it was no picnic. Twenty years supporting the family. He was either in the barn with that damned boat or at the Blue Spruce. And then he takes off for three years and when he comes back everything is supposed to be just great." Then she stiffened, looked directly at me, and said, "A person can only take so much, ya know."

She's living out in the farmhouse, which was awarded to her in the divorce settlement. She is back to being alone and brave and often speculates darkly about what Lamont might be "up to now" in the Cities.

Sherry Moves Home for a While

It's only the end of June and it's too warm too soon. When the summer ripens, the heat will make people irritable and lethargic. By the middle of August the heat waves rising off the cornfields will make the horizon wiggle and the dogs will be moving slow and even the most sweet-tempered children will have gone whiny.

But before the irritability and lethargy comes a short period of garnered courage in the face of this cyclical adversity. You dig your Bermuda shorts out of the back of the closet and get the window fans out of the basement and buy a twelve-pack of Popsicles for the kids and tell yourself that this isn't so bad. Which works until it's too hot for any clothes and the fan blows hot air like a hair dryer and the Popsicles are all over the faces and front halves of the kids.

Courage is followed by indulgence; in this stage you permit yourself not to do a whole host of chores that you ought to do because, well, it's just too hot. You begin to indulge the children because it's too hot to argue. In time, you permit most anything, as long as they stay outside and don't touch you or anything valuable with their sticky paws. If summer lasted any longer than it does, civilization as we know it, all order and discipline, would sink into a miasma of laziness and permissiveness.

It was hot this past Sunday in church. Attendance was thin, as it usually is in the heat. This, of course, is a particularly visible manifestation of the summer decline of civilization. The building is not air-conditioned, but we have woven wicker hand fans donated and placed in the pew racks by the Howe Funeral Home some forty years ago. As the congregation fans itself through the sermon, they look like troubled water—restless, agitated, and eager to go.

Sitting with Angus and Minnie MacDowell in the third pew on the pulpit side was their son, Larry, from Spokane. On either side of Larry sat his four-year-old and his three-year-old. They were all fanning vigorously. Not sitting or fanning anywhere was their wife and mother, Sherry. Larry is forty-something. Late childbearing seems to run in the family. MacDowells enter into nothing lightly or unadvisedly.

Sherry's absence ached for an explanation, but something about the family mood induced congregational discretion. All through coffee hour, nobody asked what everybody was thinking: "Well, where *is* Sherry, anyway?"

As everybody drifted to the parking lot and that sweet taste of air-conditioning on the ride home, Minnie sneaked up on me, tugged at my sleeve, and said in a near-whisper: "Pastor, could I see you in your study?" I looked at Angus, who was watching this out of the corner of his eye.

Minnie sat on the front six inches of the vinyl chair in my office, her back straight as she held the bulletin from the worship service, which she had managed to roll up into a tight little tube. As she talked, she worked at rolling it even tighter. She and Angus were just back from Spokane, she said, where they had gone to visit Larry and Sherry and the grandchildren. They had planned on staying for two and a half weeks, but came home after one. "You see, Pastor," she said, "there was a problem."

The bulletin in her hands was now about the diameter of a pencil. These, I knew, were very large words for Minnie MacDowell, who, in general, had simply not permitted problems in her family. And if there were problems, they were certainly not called such and were never talked about to others. For Minnie to say "there was a problem" was akin to most people dropping to their knees, tearing at their clothing, and sobbing about hopelessness, guilt, and possible suicide. Minnie knew her Bible, of course, and knew that "all have sinned and fallen short of the glory of God." But she did not understand these words in a *personal* sense, but rather in a general one, as in "People in *general* have sinned and fallen short," some people much more than others, and Minnie had well-formed ideas about who. So for Minnie to say "there was a problem" was a confession of apocalyptic proportion. The problem, of course, was that Sherry, seven months pregnant, and mother of two, had not been in the third pew on the pulpit side that morning. Sherry was, Minnie revealed in a cathartic burst, "in Mankato, staying with her folks."

"Could you talk to her, Pastor? Ask her to call Larry." And then, looking at her bulletin-tube, she went on, "Tell her I'm sorry if I said anything." With those last words, all of southwestern Minnesota trembled.

Words had been spoken, and Minnie had spoken them. "What happened?" I asked. "Well," Minnie said, "it was really hot in Spokane, too, and Angus and I were there only five days when the baby got the chicken pox. Angus and Larry thought that it would be helpful if they just sort of got out of the way, so they went bowling on Thursday, and while they were gone the water heater quit and when they got back Larry went to fix it and we were watching him go into the crawl space to look at it, and we were talking about how good Larry has always been with mechanical matters and I think I said something that may have hurt Sherry's feelings a little. Well, when Larry emerged from the crawl space, she handed him the baby, went upstairs to the bedroom, locked the door, called the airlines, and bought a one-way ticket to Mankato. All she said to Larry was

'Don't call me, I'll call you, and there's another box of oatmeal bath under the sink in the children's bathroom.' "

"What was it you said, Minnie?" I asked.

"Well, I don't remember exactly," she answered. "Something about fixing the water heater." The failure of her memory at this point stood in intriguing contrast to her precise memory of Sherry's last words.

"I've got to go to Mankato on Tuesday," I said. "I'll stop and see Sherry."

She was happy to see me. Seven months pregnant, she negotiated her way onto the plastic-covered couch in her parents' fussy living room, took a sip of iced tea, and asked if I had seen Larry and the kids and how were they? How was Jered's chicken pox? Had the pox crusted over yet? Was he sleeping through the night?

"How are you?" I asked. There were a few tears as she told her tale, which was commonplace enough: how she stopped working when Jessica was born, not because she had to but because she really wanted to be home with the baby, day-to-day life with two preschoolers whom she loved as life itself. "But there are days, Dave, when I think I might forget how to talk in complete sentences. Diapers . . . ear infections . . . reading *The Cat in the Hat* fourteen times in one afternoon . . . who hit whom first. You don't even get to go to the bathroom alone. I love them so, but I can hardly wait till they go to sleep at night, and then I'm so tired I can't move."

She pulled her pregnant self up a bit. "And now number three . . . I don't know if I'll make it." She paused for a second, took another sip of iced tea, and went on: "Dave, what I didn't need was two weeks with Larry's folks. We've always gotten on but it was the straw that broke the camel's back. They're so, well . . . THERE! No salt in the food. Angus patrols the house with a screwdriver and a hammer fixing things. The kids get to them. And then Minnie . . ."

With that she looked away and her eyes reddened. "Oh, I don't know, maybe I'm overreacting. No sooner does their plane land than Jered gets the chicken pox. He's up all night. I'm up all night. Larry sleeps like a brick. Has to work the next morning, you know. Things were edgy by Thursday. Larry says that it might help if he got Dad out of the house, so they go bowling—bowling in air-conditioning. Did I tell you how hot it was? Anyway, I go to give the baby another oatmeal bath and the water comes out like ice. The hot-water heater picks this particular moment in the history of the world to die. I'm ready to call the plumber, but Minnie says, 'Wait till Larry gets back. I'm sure he'll be able to repair it without such an expense. You know what a talent he has for these things.'

"So no oatmeal bath and we wait for Larry and Angus to finish a third game. Larry comes home and says, 'If I'd known that the thing was going to bust, we would have never gone, honey.' Somehow that didn't help. The hot-water heater is in a crawl space under the kitchen. It's hard to get to. You have to go in about twenty feet on your hands and knees. Anyway, Angus and Minnie and I are watching Larry's rear end as he makes his way to the water heater. Jered is in my arms whining and Jessica is wiping Oreo off her face with my skirt. There's a moment of quiet as Larry gets up to the hot-water heater, and then Minnie says to me— David, I still can't believe she said it—she says, 'Sherry, it's really a good thing that you didn't lose that weight, or Larry might have had you crawl in there.'

"Something snapped, Dave. It had never crossed my mind to walk out on them. Family deserters are scum you read about in the *Star*. But it was just so much, just so much. . . ."

We talked another hour. I didn't have to talk her into coming down to North Haven to make peace. She had already called Larry that afternoon. Nothing I said was needed to persuade her to go home with them to Spokane. That was always what she was going to do.

I think Minnie's tongue was tamed in all of this, which it needed. I think Larry and maybe even Angus have seen something of Sherry's world from her vantage point, which they needed. And of course, Sherry got a break, which she needed.

Life together is hard. There are no perfect husbands, no perfect wives, no perfect children, no perfect mothers-in-law. Life in family—life in any community—is both our sorest test and our sweetest joy. Life together stretches us, pulls us, strains us, but in it we are nourished by the struggle itself.

It is the best chance Providence gives most of us to grow out of ourselves and into something more like what we were meant to be. Life together is the welcome tether that kindly but relentlessly binds our ravenous egos. Life together is where most people get their only chance to be heroes. Families can breed heroes—local heroes, yes, but giants of spirit nevertheless: courageous and well-tempered souls who return again and again to brave the rigors and savor the delicacies of loving the same people for a long time. For the only thing harder than getting along with other people is getting along without them, even Minnie.

Air-Conditioning

A week before we went on vacation the furnace in the manse died. The church owns the house, so it was their worry. The day the furnace dies is one of the few times when it is a happy thing to be living in a house that belongs to somebody else.

I called Arnie Peterson, who is head of the Board of Trustees these days, and he called up Jimmy Wilcox, who runs the only heating business in the county. Arnie set up a meeting for the three of us the next morning at nine-thirty in the basement of the manse. Coffee cups in our hands, we stood around the old furnace like an anxious family at the bedside of a dying grandparent. With a flashlight in one hand and a three-foot stick in the other, Jimmy peered and poked into the innards of the ancient hot-air monster. The thing looked like a giant octopus standing on its head, its tentacles grasping the bottom of the joists of the first floor of the house.

Like a discreet doctor, Jimmy guided us away from the presence of the patient over to the foot of the basement steps before he offered a prognosis, which was terminal. He said softly, "Thing's been on its last legs as long as anybody can remember. There's no fixin' her." Furnaces are all female to Jimmy, like boats are female to sailors and cars are female to mechanics. "Church is just gonna have to spring for a new one." We all knew as much, but with his next words, Jimmy opened a can of worms: "Tell ya what I'll do. For about five hundred bucks more, I'll put in one of these new heat pumps instead of a regular furnace. That's at cost, of course. Then in the summer, Pastor and his family can have air-conditioning. You see, these heat pumps cool in the summer and heat in the winter."

"Air-conditioning." The very word bespoke pleasure and danger. I imagined cool, restful nights with the windows closed against the often torturous heat of July. I sensed danger when I imagined the words "air-conditioning" and "manse" appearing in the same sentence at a trustees meeting. I decided to be cautiously supportive. "That would be nice but . . ." I said, my first and last utterance on the topic.

I had been raised in an upper-middle-class and slightly warmer world where air-conditioning was assumed to be as much a necessity of life as central heating. It was a comfort that had always just been there, a flick of the thermostat away. When we arrived in North Haven we had been mildly surprised to discover that neither the church nor the manse had air-conditioning. When I once inquired about this curiosity, the reply was "Don't really need it so far north, usually." We discovered that "usually" is about eleven months of the year. But the one month that falls outside of "usually" can be hell. Maybe a lifetime of breathing conditioned air had atrophied whatever heat-enduring strength I had been born with. Or perhaps it was the fact that it is so seldom terribly hot here. But, in any case, the middle two weeks of this past July, with a string of nights never below 85 degrees, had reduced me to a sweaty lump of irritable lethargy. I wanted air-conditioning.

Jimmy, bless his persistent soul, wouldn't let go of the heat pump idea and convinced Arnie, who likes new gadgets and has air-conditioning in his house, that the heat pump was the way to go. The trustees were to meet later that week at the church to decide on the matter.

It was, unfortunately, a cool and comfortable evening. Everyone arrived knowing all the details about the matter at hand. Only Arnie was a declared heat pump man. Bob Beener is the newest and youngest trustee. He's about thirty, half the age of most of the others, and is tiresomely zealous in his trusteeship. In preparation for the meeting, he had conducted a one-man random-sample survey of the church membership and summarized his findings in a three-page document, plastic-bound copies of which he circulated to the board. It was entitled: "Varieties and Distribution of Home Cooling Technologies Among the Membership of Second Presbyterian Church, North Haven, Minn.: A Survey." Bob had been to col-

lege and knew that two-part titles divided by a co-
lon bore great authority.

There was a full page describing his methodol-
ogy and then a few disclaimers about statistical
projection, all of which meant that some folks
weren't home when he called or had told him it
was none of his business and he was making a
good guess. On page three was the meat of the
matter: 45 percent of church homes had electric
fans ("window and/or oscillating"), 38 percent
had window air-conditioning units ("one or
more"), 12 percent had whole house air-conditioning or heat pumps, and 5 percent sweated it
out with nothing.

The more they talked about it, the more angles
there were. Clearly, air-conditioning was contro-
versial. "If we're gonna air-condition anything,"
Bob suggested, "we should start with the church."
Opinions were offered as to air-conditioning and
health problems ("causes summer colds") and ben-
efits ("for folks with allergies").

But the unspoken text was the shared cultural
assumption that air-conditioning was a moral issue. There was the "fairness" question: Is it proper
for the minister to be one of the elite 12 percent?
But far deeper was the bred-in-the-bone conviction
shared by most in little Minnesota towns that air-
conditioning is fundamentally decadent, a wimpy
urban extravagance appropriate only as an indulgence for the weak. Summers are short, money is
tight, and these are people weaned on a Nordic
stoicism that knows you can die from the cold

here, but not from the heat. When Angus allowed that he had only had it put in his house because of Minnie's bouts with hay fever, the case for whole-house air-conditioning in the manse was closed.

But these are sweet folks and they know how hot the second floor of a house can get in the unusual months of July and August, so a compromise was reached. Instead of spending the extra $500 on the heat pump, they voted to put in a regular furnace and buy two window A/C units for the upstairs bedrooms. These two units ended up costing $300 apiece, but they were noncontroversial (38 percent of all church members owned one or more). Everybody went home happy, even though there seemed to be a lingering awareness that the logic behind the decision was less than consistent. I went home and told Annie that we should load up the car and leave early the next morning for vacation. She didn't ask about air-conditioning.

Vacation was gracious oblivion, a respite from clocks and telephones and vocation. This year we went north to Nisswa, Minnesota, the other side of Brainerd, for two weeks in a rented cottage at Sundquist's Singing Sand Resort on the grassy shores of Pelican Lake. We got up late and made egg-coffee and waffles. Annie and I sat in the painted metal lawn chairs, read paperbacks, and watched the kids splash in the lake. Late in the afternoon, we fished for sunnies off the end of the dock with a drop line and angleworms. In the evening, we put on orange kapok lifejackets and circled the lake in the aluminum boat named only *Cabin 3* with its five-horse Evinrude. Often I didn't know what day it was and the phone never rang. At night, we made love very quietly so as not to wake the kids, whose breathing we could hear through the knotty-pine partition that separated the head of their beds from ours.

When we returned home, we walked right into the arms of one of the great church doings of the year: "The Annual August P. W. (Presbyterian Women) Chicken Bar-B-Q," which is held in the town park next door to the church. It has been held right after services on the last Sunday in August since as long as anybody can remember.

We all sat at folding tables eating three-bean salad and smelling the chicken that the Men's Bowling Team was roasting over the cinder block barbecue pit. The air-conditioning business was still in the back of my mind. Annie and I had still not talked much about it, but the silliness of it was somehow emblematic of so much of the silliness of life in general. Sitting next to Angus and across from Bob Beener, and not wanting to talk about it, I asked, "How did things go the Sundays we were gone?"

"Slow," Angus said, "slow. It's been hot. Last Sunday was hot. Nobody told you yet what happened, Dave?" The preacher for the last two Sundays had been the Reverend Mr. Tuttle, a retired Baptist whose low energy level, kindly and mild manners, and, now, great age, have conspired to make it impossible for him to be that which he has long desired to be, namely a spellbinder, save-the-socks-off-of-'em-"Amen, brother!" Baptist preacher.

"What happened?" I asked.

"Well," Angus said, pushing his paper plate of chicken bones away from him. "It was hot, never even got cool Saturday night. By ten o'clock Sunday morning, it was hotter than Hades in the sanctuary. Well, you know what I mean. All the windows in the church were wide open, everybody was dripping wet, fanning themselves, hoping for the least breath of air.

"Reverend Tuttle was preaching on the topic 'Be Ye Prepared.' He meant prepared for judgment. We were prepared for him to be finished. He told us that he dare not shorten a sermon on account of heat, for this was but a hint of what was to come for the unprepared. What with all the windows wide open, a grasshopper had got himself into the church, one of those big greeny-brown ones about three inches long. This old grasshopper somehow ended up perched on the railing in front of the choir loft up in the front. It was hot for him, too, I suppose, and he just sat there for the longest time, watching the choir, the choir watching him."

Our choir is just nine folks: eight lady sopranos and one gentleman who sings various parts as needed. Angus sipped iced tea from a foam cup and went on. "Every now and again, the grasshopper would sort of fidget, and the ladies in the choir would gasp and scooch down a bit in their pew. They knew he was going to jump any minute. He was getting prepared and the choir was getting prepared, just like the Reverend Tuttle was saying in his sermon.

"He was winding up with this description of the fate of the unprepared. He went to draw a breath, and that grasshopper jumped, jumped right into the middle of the choir loft. The whole choir leaped up and threw their arms in the air and screeched and started shaking their robes to make sure the grasshopper wasn't in there. Pastor, it was a fine sight for a slow Sunday morning. Well, the Reverend Tuttle was stunned. He had not seen the grasshopper and all, and concluded that it was his hellfire that had succeeded in gettin' the choir all excited. He looked over at 'em leaping around the choir loft, looked down at his sermon notes, and smiled."

Angus winked at me. Across the table Bob Beener was laughing so hard that he had tears running down his cheeks. He got control of himself and said to me, "Listening to dear old Sam Tuttle is like watching paint dry. Glad you're back."

I looked around the park at the congregation of Second Presbyterian gnawing at chicken bones and chasing cold three-bean salad around paper plates with little plastic spoons. Most all of them had lived lives harder and leaner than my near-forty years of suburban ease. If the long bleakness of their winters, the caprice of crops and climate, and the fact that they stayed when others left had bred a resolute pride in them that disdained air-conditioning, they were to be forgiven, even loved, for it. The hot weather was past and the 38 percent of us who had one or more window units would probably not be needing them again till next summer. I was glad to be back.

The Treasure Hunt

When we returned from Nisswa, I found a stack of unopened mail on my desk about eighteen inches high. Next to it was a much smaller pile of a couple dozen "While You Were Out" message memos from Maureen, the church secretary. Each one represented a call, a visit, or a meeting that I would have to make in the next week or two. There was no way that I was going to have any time for the Kaffe Fest this year, no matter how much Christopher wanted to go.

Most everyone in town still calls the annual community celebration held the first few days of September the "Kaffe Fest" (pronounced "Coffee Fest"). Officially, it is billed as "Summerfest '90" or whatever the year happens to be. The Jaycees came up with this latter name after the less popular "Soybean Festival" was married to the more popular "Kaffe Fest" six or eight years ago. It seems as though pulling off two big celebrations in town every year was stretching the local organizers a little thin. One big town festivity instead of two feeble ones seemed just the thing.

But the new name coined for this marriage sounded contrived in most everybody's ears and never really stuck. The old Soybean Festival had originated as the brainchild of some boosterish County Extension Officer back in the fifties when soybeans began to be a popular crop with local farmers. He was convinced that soy-everything was the wave of the future and proposed a festival to raise the public image of what is admittedly an unromantic agricultural product. In the early years there was a parade featuring children dressed as soybeans and a beauty pageant climaxing in the coronation of "The Queen of the Bean" and her "Soy-al Court" (all of the runners-up). There were contests for the growers (best yield per acre, most promising new hybrid, etc.), and contests for the best recipe featuring soy meal (never a wildly successful event).

The Kaffe Fest was born in the prohibition battles of the twenties as a counterpoint to festivals in general, which had historically featured stronger stuff than coffee. The local Swedes and Norwegians, most of whom equated the Volstead Act with the coming of the Kingdom, were particularly keen on this celebration of their favorite beverage, hence the Scandinavian spelling. The chief feature of the Kaffe Fest had always been the closing off of Main Street from Jefferson to Jackson and the construction of one four-block-long table. From eight to five Monday through Friday coffee is served at a nickel a cup to locals who consume it (black, sometimes with sugar) in even greater quantities than usual. They down cup after cup, ruminate about the weather, and speculate about the size of this year's Kaffe Fest crowd as compared to last year.

So at the end of each summer, we crown the Queen of the Bean (soy or coffee, take your pick). A parade marches down Main Street, and we gather for the four-block caffeine binge. Two years ago the Jaycees invited McQuade's Mobile Concessions and Entertainments ("the cleanest show in Minnesota"), featuring half a dozen assorted thrill rides such as the Tilt-O-Whirl, the Scrambler, the Bullet. The alertness induced by the eight cups of coffee you have had since lunch sharpen the experience of riding on these machines.

Last year the Jaycees introduced yet another element to "Summerfest '89": a treasure hunt. On the radio every morning at eight for the week of the Kaffe Fest, just after the St. Paul stock market report, Bob Schlict reads a "clue" handed to him "just this morning in a sealed envelope" by a member of the North Haven Jaycees. Bob is the host of the "Sun's Up, What's Up?" morning show on KZRT AM and FM ("The Voice of the Valley"). This clue is a more or less cryptic intimation as to the location of the "Treasure Box of the Day, hidden somewhere in or near North Haven, Minnesota." In each box is a fifty-dollar gift certificate donated by a local merchant.

Providentially, I was too busy to consider participation in such adventure. All Sunday afternoon, Christopher pleaded with me to drive him around to help him look for the treasure. I tried to explain to him how busy I was. Christopher is my seven-year-old son. Last June he "flunked first grade." That's how he puts it, not how Miss Lillian, his teacher, put it. She used all the right words about "rates of development" and "boys sometimes getting off to a slower start." Actually, he just can't read yet. Annie and I exuded concern and cooperation to cover up for the knot of fear and embarrassment we both felt as parents. Miss Lillian said, "Work with him over the summer."

Work with him I did. And it was agony for both of us. We went over sounds and letters, and then over them again, as if these "rules" would help much in the crazy world of English spelling. When it came time to try to read, Chris would always choose the same three books. I realized after two weeks that he had the words memorized. We found new books, and during my vacation we piled up hour upon frustrating hour. Often our session ended up with me angry and him in tears. About two weeks ago, halfway through vacation, Annie called a halt to the lessons.

School had never been hard for me, and I could not shake the impression that Chris's problem was somehow related to "not trying hard enough," as though real effort on his part would suddenly break what was still to him a puzzling code of secret symbols. Vacation up north had ended with a strain in our relationship. He was tense in my presence, as if my love for him were suddenly qualified by his "flunking" of first grade. And though I would have denied it, I was simply disappointed in him. For an hour Sunday afternoon he sat on the edge of the sofa where I was reading the Sunday *Star and Tribune.* He sat in silence until I put one section aside and rummaged for another. Then he would look at me until I returned his gaze and just say, "Please." Suddenly I heard his insistence as an appeal to ease the discomfort we had both been feeling. He would only be seven once. And a lot of those "While You Were Out" memos would keep.

Everyone in town figured out after the first few days that this year's clues were the creations of Jasper Werzinski, a Jaycee and a backslapping fundamentalist. All five of this year's clues were biblical in nature. This odd use of Holy Scripture conforms comfortably to Jasper's manner of approaching the Bible, which he understands not so much as a story but rather as a divinely inspired puzzle—a sort of spiritual treasure hunt.

Monday morning, the first day of the Kaffe Fest, Chris and I tuned in to KZRT at eight sharp. After learning the current prices of "barrows and gilts" (down in active trading), we listened to Bob Schlict tear open the "sealed envelope" and, after what was either a pregnant or incredulous pause, read the clue: "Psalm 2, verse 3."

Christopher and I looked at each other. He said, "That's your department, Dad," implying that I really ought to know the verse off the top of my head.

"Go get your Bible, Chris!" I said as I pointed upstairs to his bedroom, "The one Great-grandpa gave you." That Bible is a King James Version, of course, which my maternal grandfather tiresomely refers to as the "real Bible." I helped Chris find the reference and put my finger on the lines for him to read.

But he looked at me pleadingly, and I read, moving my finger along for him to follow: "Let us break their bands asunder, and cast away their cords from us."

"What's it about, Dad?" he asked. I tried to think of a way to explain the ancient Babylonian domination of Israel to a seven-year-old. Then I thought better of it and said that it was about these guys who were being held prisoner by these other guys and who wanted to be free.

Chris and I discussed the possibilities in the clue. Inside of five minutes, we made a dash for the car. I drove as fast as I dared to the North Haven Police Department, which is really the back two rooms of the Town Hall. There is no jail as such, but one of those two rooms is a makeshift holding room with a metal door and heavy mesh over the window. Three cars had gotten there before us and another dozen pulled up as Chris and I and the rest of the treasure hunters riffled through the bushes. We looked inside the mailbox and poked around in the red and white petunias planted around the base of the "North Haven Police Station" sign.

At one point I looked sheepishly toward the building and saw Billy Hobart's eyes peering out through the venetian blinds. Billy is a typically nononsense cop. He turned away, shook his bald head, and headed for the door. A moment later Chief Hobart, who is in fact half the entire force, stood watching with his hands on his hips. "What the heck are you people doing?" he asked. Nobody said anything.

By the time we left, there were a good thirty-five people wandering around the back of Town Hall sniffing for treasure. We were driving home in silence, when Chris fairly screamed, "Bands! Dad, how about the bandstand at the park?"

Which was exactly where the first Treasure Box of the Day had been placed by the Jaycees. We were not the first to arrive, however. Monday's fifty-dollar gift certificate went to a brother and sister team, Danny and Amy Olson, for whom "bands" had immediately meant just that.

It took our failures to solve the Psalm-based clues of Tuesday and Wednesday to demonstrate the pointlessness of overanalysis of Jasper's hints. For instance, Tuesday's clue had been Psalm 78:46: "He gave also their increase unto the caterpillar, and their labour unto the locust." The treasure box had been under the seat of a yellow bulldozer in the County Road Department's yard on the edge of town. Good fundamentalist that he was, Jasper had no time for matters as arcane as metaphor. Everything "meant what it meant," as he would say. Bands were bands. Caterpillars were caterpillars.

Every morning that week, Chris and I would get up and have our breakfast and then listen to the "Sun's Up, What's Up?" show together. We'd laugh at Bob Schlict's lame jokes, and when it came time for the clue, Chris would hand me the pencil and the paper, climb into my lap, and put his finger to his lips as Jim read the clue for the day. He was enjoying the treasure hunt immensely.

By Thursday, however, I was getting increasingly frustrated. I was determined to outwit Jasper Werzinski. Actually, outwitting him was not so much the challenge. Thinking as literally as Jasper was the challenge.

When we dashed out of the house on Thursday, I was muttering the clue over and over to myself as Chris joyfully tagged behind. As we passed through the front door, Annie said to me, "Getting into treasure hunting, aren't we?" I feigned a mad grimace and Chris answered, "Dad and I are gonna find treasure for sure, Mom."

But Thursday saw another failure for the Battles team. The clue was Psalm 68, verse 25: "The singers went before, the players on instruments followed after . . ." Chris and I and a few dozen other hunters went to the field in back of the high school where the marching band practices. The treasure box for Thursday was found in the alley next to Betty's Knit 'n Sew ("Distributors of Singer and Bernina Sewing Machines").

Failure was playing differently on me than on Chris. By Friday I felt as though I were locked in mortal hermeneutical battle with Jasper Werzinski. I felt that Chris must think me a silly kind of minister to have been stumped four times in a row by clues from the Bible, the book about which I was supposed to be an expert. Chris, however, was simply enjoying the time in front of the radio, enjoying the time in the car, enjoying poking around the town with me for hidden treasure. He seemed undaunted by the fact that we had found nothing.

On Friday I decided that we would tune into the "Sun's Up, What's Up?" show on the car radio to give us just a little jump on things. We listened to Bob Schlict's seemingly endless banter as the time came for the last clue to be read. Chris was on my lap. I was beating the steering wheel with a pencil and growing impatient. Finally I muttered to the radio, "Good God, you fool, get on with it!" Chris looked at me quizzically and said nothing.

Bob finally got on with it and read with especially dramatic pauses the clue for Friday: "Psalm 65, verses 12 *and* 13." Chris handed me the Bible from on top of the dashboard and I read out loud: "They drop upon the pastures of the wilderness: and the little hills rejoice on every side. The pastures are clothed with flocks; the valleys also are covered over with corn; they shout for joy, they also sing."

"There's only one spot that can be, Christopher, the Hofer place." The only geographical feature in the North Haven area that could even optimistically be called a hill was Hazel Hofer's farm north of town toward the river. When we arrived, I was excited by the realization that we were the only treasure hunters at the site. "This will be the day," I said to myself. We drove the roads around the farm for about ten minutes looking for some spot where all the features of verses 12 and 13 were more or less present: "wilderness, little hills, pastures, flocks, and corn."

About a mile down County Road 18 from the Hofer driveway, I looked to the left and saw a small sign set a few feet back from the road that read: NO HUNTING, WILDERNESS WETLANDS REFUGE. I looked to the right and saw a large cornfield and behind the field, rising like Zion, that ridge on the north edge of the Hofer farm that is our only hill. We had just passed a pasture with sheep grazing in it. "This is the place, Christopher," I said.

For an hour we wandered up and down the road. We poked through the high grass along the shoulder of the road and searched the area around the Refuge sign with special thoroughness. Leaning against the car for a rest, I noticed that if I positioned myself even with the "wilderness" sign and looked north to the highest point of the ridge (the "little hills"), my line of sight went straight down a row in the middle of the cornfield. "It's got to be out there," I said to Chris. It never occurred to me that whoever was leasing Hazel Hofer's land would not be pleased with treasure hunters traipsing through a field of soon to be harvested corn. I told Chris to wait by the car while I walked into the cornfield.

A stand of field corn in late summer is much like a dense forest. The stalks are a good seven or eight feet tall. The rows of corn are close together and you have to almost push your way through the sharp foliage as though it were jungle. But it's easy to stay oriented because the corn is sown in long neat rows. To get out you simply retrace your steps back down a corn row.

But about two hundred yards into the field, the rows changed direction. I suppose I should have walked back to the car by the the same row or the one to the right or to the left. I was so sure I was close to Friday's treasure. I went into the next field and pushed my way across the rows toward the "little hills" that I could no longer see. Suddenly the direction of the planting switched again, not 90 degrees as they had the last time, but maybe 45. Whoever had planted this corn was using the slight contour of the land to best advantage. After about forty-five minutes, I had still not come out on the other side of the field as I expected I would. I decided to return to the car where Chris was probably getting anxious.

I turned back down the row I was in and walked till the direction of the planting changed direction. I looked to my right and to my left down the row I had come to. I walked a few paces down it to the right, stopped, and thought, *No, I turned to my left the first time the rows changed, and to the right the second time . . . or was it the other way around?* There was no point of reference. The day was overcast, hiding the sun. There was no way to see over the eight-foot cornstalks. The slight roll of the land confused me. I started to walk across the rows, pushing my way through the sharp and brittle foliage. Every row looked like every other row. Every stalk of corn was identical to every other. I was moving faster and faster, almost running, turning a number of times down rows that looked somehow familiar. It took me a few moments to realize that I was lost. I stopped to think, and what I thought of was Christopher, for whom rows of words on a page were as labyrinthine and mysterious as this cornfield was for me.

For those who have never ventured into a large stand of mature corn, the idea of being lost there seems impossible and absurd. But it is possible and I was feeling quite absurd. And I was just at the edge of frightened, not so much for myself, but for Christopher. The control implicit in knowing what direction is what is snatched from you. You do not know whether you are walking swiftly toward or away from your child waiting alone by the car.

But this anxiety was mixed with the larger question of how I was going to keep Chris from relating this story to his mother, who would not approve of my leaving a seven-year-old alone in the country, but would certainly enjoy the tale of my getting lost in a cornfield. I knew I would eventually emerge from the field onto one of the roads that surrounded it. "Eventually" could be this afternoon, however.

As that thought struck me, I heard the car horn honk. Three short blasts followed by silence and then three more. The pattern repeated itself, and I knew that somebody must have come across Christopher, who was probably in tears, and asked him where his daddy was. Concluding that the Presbyterian preacher from back East had gotten himself lost in a cornfield, they sat down to honk their horn as a beacon for me.

I followed the sound and came to the edge of the field around the corner and a half mile down the road from where I had left Chris. As I approached the corner, I expected to see a dozen cars. They would have called Annie, who would be holding her son, eyes reddened by tears, head on her shoulder. She would shake her head at me in disbelief. Maybe Billy Hobart would be there with the lights on the squad car flashing. The crowd would be watching me with their arms folded in front of them. Billy would speak into his radio microphone and say, "Call it off, George, we got him."

But as I rounded the corner and looked down the road, I saw only our blue Ford Taurus and, through the windshield, the top of Chris's head. He was sitting in the driver's seat, honking the horn at intervals. When he saw me, he scrambled out of the car and, leaving the door open, ran to me, jumped into my arms, and said, "Dad, I found you!"

On our way home, we drove around to the other side of the field in which I had been lost The north side of the field runs along County Road 19, which rises slightly as it skirts the edge of the "little hills." From that rise you can look across the field to the "wilderness" where we had been parked. Danny Olson found Friday's treasure box at the high point of the road. It was sitting in plain sight in the gravel of the berm. It contained a fifty-dollar J. C. Penney gift certificate. This time we had at least been warm.

Chris was in high spirits, proud of himself for honking the horn for me. And I was proud of him and surprised that the idea had come to him. He was also relieved, of course. And I was relieved when he said, "Let's not tell Mom about this." He moved over to the middle of the seat and put his left arm onto my shoulder. "I sure love treasure hunting," my son said. "Can we do it again next year?"

We had both found treasure, of course, in being lost together, I in the corn, he in his letters. I'm sure we will do it again next year. In fact, maybe he and I will start to hunt treasure all the time. So often, the treasures that life hides from us are to be found not at the end of the search, but in the searching itself, especially when you look together.

The Dreadful Omniscience of God

Last week's Presbytery meeting in Mankato was a vaguely uncomfortable one. It was all entirely polite, of course. People here are agonizingly polite and restrained, and talk on touchy topics is wonderfully circuitous. A raised voice is looked upon as a manifestation of poor self-discipline—behavior typical of spoiled children and people who live too near one of the coasts of this country. Difficult conversations are conducted in a slow and deliberate voice. Generally, the slower and more softly you speak the angrier you are. Everybody understands this, so it works well. But it can be mystifying, to say the least, to someone like me who grew up too near one of the oceans and who actually has seen unrelated people yelling at each other.

An outside observer to that Presbytery meeting

would have never guessed that any but a cordial felicity was the order of the day. The Presbytery voted upon the dissolution of the pastoral relationship between the Reverend Mitchell Simpson and the Johnston Memorial Presbyterian Church in St. Paul. First we heard a brief report of the congregational meeting at which the church voted to accept the Reverend Simpson's resignation. The first hint of an unspoken subtext to these proceedings occurred when the neighboring minister, who had moderated this congregational meeting, said, "A quorum being present, the congregation voted eighty-seven to three to accept the pastor's resignation." What was wrong was what he didn't say. He didn't say "voted *with regret* to accept the pastor's resignation." The congregation always votes "with regret" to accept the pastor's resignation, even if they've been trying to get rid of him for ten years.

Next there were two polite but carefully worded speeches by a couple of elders from Johnston Memorial. One said that the Reverend Simpson's children would be missed in the youth group, and the other made veiled remarks about "our former pastor's many challenging new ideas and his unique candor and ever-present frankness." Even people at the Presbytery meeting who didn't know the real story were starting to listen.

Next it was Mitch Simpson's turn to say the requisite words of lament and farewell. Mitch is from New Jersey and was not raised in this culture of circumlocution. His speech was unusually brief.

In his three years in the Presbytery, Mitch came to be known as a maker of frequent and indignant speeches, often raising his voice and making actual gestures with his hands. But this time Mitch spoke in even tones and kept his hands at his sides. He said his family would miss the Twin Cities, that the three years really seemed much longer than that, and then he said good-bye.

What Mitch would really have liked to say is that he wished that wireless microphones had never been invented. But the incident with the wireless microphone was not the real problem, even though Mitch thought it was.

The real problem was that Johnston Memorial Presbyterian Church and the Reverend Mitchell Simpson were an incredible mismatch. This had become apparent to everyone except Mitch in the space of about a month. Johnston Memorial is an aging—in fact, aged—congregation possessed of a magnificent stone building unhappily located between a new freeway and an old set of railroad tracks. Warehouses lie to one side, downtown St. Paul to the other. The neighborhood that built the church went from "residential" to "commercial and mixed" thirty years ago, and most everybody moved out, including the Mr. Johnston who built the warehouses and paid for most of the church building. It is a dying church, and all it needed was and is a loving pastor to do a lot of funerals and to let the church slip gracefully into history.

But Mitch Simpson came fresh out of seminary,

gripped by a vision. This was a vision not so much of an invigorated Johnston Memorial Church, but more a vision of the Reverend Mitchell Simpson, dynamic young clergyman who turns around a dying downtown church. The members of Johnston Memorial, every last one of whom is retired, were wise to the ways of all flesh and saw the hubris at the root of Mitch's energy. When Mitch's proud vision of pastoral triumph failed to materialize, he took to scolding the congregation in his sermons. They took it stoically. But it only took the wireless microphone to bring this unfortunate union to an end.

The wireless mike was, rumor has it, Mitch's idea. It was hardly necessary, as the back half of the church had been roped off to make everybody sit up front. The old pulpit mike worked fine. But a wireless mike represented cutting-edge technology for the church and was somehow part of Mitch Simpson's vision of his destiny as a clergyman.

Now, these gadgets work like this: you wear a tiny microphone on your lapel and a wire connects it to a transmitter hitched to your belt; a two-foot antenna dangles down your side. All this sends whatever the mike picks up to a receiver in the storage room at the back of the church. The receiver is connected to the speakers in the sanctuary. The preacher can then roam from pulpit to communion table and up and down the aisle without any wires connecting him to anything and still be amplified in the whole church.

The instruction booklet noted in bold letters that THE USER MUST TAKE CAUTION TO ACTIVATE ON/ OFF SWITCH ON UNIT ONLY WHEN READY TO BROADCAST. The on/off switch was, however, very small and not clearly visible when attached to the user's belt. The Sunday after it arrived in the mail, Mitch wired himself up, put on his robe, and reached inside to check the switch on the unit hooked to his belt. He pushed it down, which for most switches means off, but not for this one.

As the congregation of Johnston Memorial waited for the service to begin that day, the first odd sound they heard was the rustling of papers as Mitch shuffled through notes in his office. Then Mitch, it seems, finished shuffling and took one last look out his window. He saw a middle-aged couple he knew to be from the Congregational church on the other side of the freeway. That church was in the middle of a grand battle over something or other and folk were reputed to be leaving in droves. Mitch opened his office door, which caused the entire congregation to look up at the ceiling speakers. Mitch saw an elder walking down the hall toward the church and called out to him, "Sam, the Bengtsons from the Congregational church are coming in the front door. I want you to go and make nice to 'em." As Sam marched off, Mitch muttered the fatal words to himself and to an attentively listening congregation: "Maybe a few mad Congregationalists can breathe some life into this corpse."

Now, Mitch had drunk four cups of coffee that

morning and the next thing he did was to walk to the washroom, open the door, do what he needed to do, flush, walk out, shut the door, and sigh deeply. All of this, of course, was clearly audible to the stunned congregation. The full range of Mitch's humanity, physical and spiritual, had been broadcast to his entire congregation. A less prideful person could have laughed with the church, who would have been more than willing to do so. Oh, they laughed, most of St. Paul laughed, but not with Mitch. Mitch Simpson was not a man to abide humor at the expense of his great pride. Being who he was, he decided to resign.

Driving home to North Haven from the Presbytery meeting, I got to thinking of all the things I have said that I wouldn't want the world to hear. Then I got to thinking of all the things that I have thought that I certainly wouldn't want the world to know. Words uttered before thought, angry words, vain thoughts, idle thoughts, stupid thoughts, all the things that I would not want another to know.

A verse from the 139th Psalm came to mind: "O Lord, thou hast searched me and known me! . . . Thou discernest my thoughts from afar . . . and art acquainted with all my ways. Even before a word is on my tongue, lo, O Lord, thou knowest it altogether."

The Psalmist is saying that we are all fitted with a wireless mike patched into the divine mind. And the on/off switch is always "on." This image, pressing itself on my mind along U.S. 169, terrified me for a moment: To be altogether known. Every thought known. Every passion known. Every moment of doubt and jealousy known. Every motivation—the real motivation—known.

Mitch Simpson crumbled when fifty-seven elderly Presbyterians became for a moment accidentally omniscient. They overheard a bitter lament over his dying church and then heard him go about his physical necessities. The daunting awareness that rushed over me was that the One who hurled the planets into place knows absolutely everything about me—most of it much more damaging than Mitch's revelations. The omniscience of God is a dreadful thing. I prefer my privacy. I prefer the liberty of saying one thing while thinking another and getting away with it. But if I am to be known to my depths, if Mitch Simpson is to be known even more deeply than he came to be known that Sunday, it is this same God whom I would have know us. For God is even more gracious than the gentle congregation of Johnston Memorial. For the very One who knows all is the very One who forgives all. All is known, and all is forgiven . . . all is known, and all is forgiven.

The Jefferson
Street Leaf War

Even though it's only four blocks from the manse, I generally drive to the church in the evenings. Annie usually doesn't need the car, and I like to hurry home. But Tuesday night of last week I walked. It was a warm October evening—warm in contrast to the cold nights we'd been having for nearly a month. The first frost had come the last week of September.

The Tuesday Evening Bible Class has been studying the Old Testament prophets this fall. We just finished Jeremiah. The text we had discussed that night was Jeremiah, chapter 31, verses 31 to 35. The prophets, Jeremiah especially, verbally barrage the children of Israel for their failure to obey the law that bound the people to this God who cared desperately about right and wrong.

But in the thirty-first chapter of Jeremiah, the most wild-eyed of all the prophets takes a desperate step beyond the familiar theme. "The days are coming," he has God say, "when I will make a new covenant . . . not like the covenant which I made with their fathers . . . I will put my law within them, and I will write it upon their hearts . . ."

I mused on all this as I passed the tiny white bungalow on Jefferson Street that has been home to Alvina Johnson for nearly fifty years. Until last year, Alvina had been director of the church's Christmas Pageant. The house is immaculately kept, both inside and out. Alvina has managed to keep fifty-year-old furniture, carpet, even wallpaper, looking impeccable, if slightly faded, near the windows where she has been unable to police the entry of the sun's rays.

Her small lawn is weed-free. She somehow makes each blade of grass stand up straight. On each side of the front steps, standing at attention in front of the foundation, Alvina plants a row of marigolds, fourteen on each side. A sidewalk leads directly to the concrete steps and divides the front yard in half. Squarely in the middle of each side is an old tire painted white and made into a planter. In each she plants seven more marigolds, six in a circle and one in the center. It's always been this way as long as anybody can remember. The entire yard is surrounded by a picket fence about three feet high.

As I approached her house that Tuesday night, it was too dark to appreciate any of what might still remain in late October of Alvina's careful ordering of nature. But it was not too dark to see a figure moving about the yard in the shadows cast by the autumn moon. The silhouette was bending over, as if looking for something on the ground. Then it stood up, lifted a half-bushel basket, and walked toward the fence separating Alvina's yard from the Lundins' next door. It then dumped the contents of the basket over the fence into the Lundins' yard. I recognized Alvina as she shook the last of the leaves out of the basket.

I cleared my throat and walked as noisily as I could to warn Alvina of my approach. She looked up, recognized me, quickly set the little basket down, and began to remove her canvas gardening gloves. "Alvina," I said, "you're working late." It was, after all, a quarter past eleven. Every house on Jefferson Street, Alvina's included, was dark. "Snow'll be here soon, Pastor." she answered. "You know you should really get everything cleaned while you can."

I looked pointedly at the pile of leaves she had just added to on the Lundins' side of the fence. I didn't need to say anything. It was so obviously odd, even for Alvina, to be raking leaves in the dark and dumping them into the neighbors' yard.

"They're the Lundins' leaves," she said. "They're off their big oak over there." She pointed an accusatory finger at the red oak behind me in the Lundins' front yard. "The slightest breeze from the west, and half of them blow into my property. I know they belong to them because I only have the one maple in the back. I sort them out, of course; I mean, I keep all the maple leaves.

I figure they're mostly mine. But the oak lea.
theirs. It's only fair, Pastor."

There was an edge of defensiveness in Alvina
voice. If she'd been altogether comfortable with
this bizarre justice, she would hardly be executing
it just before midnight, when all the other people
on Jefferson Street—most notably the Lundins—
were in their beds. It was late and I could think of
nothing to say but "Good night, Alvina. Don't
work too hard." I told Annie about it in the
morning and we agreed that Mr. Johnson had
chosen wisely in moving to Minneapolis forty-
nine years ago.

I should not have been surprised when three
days later Alvina knocked at my office door and
asked if she could "have a moment." She removed
her hat, gloves, and coat, and sat decisively in the
chair on the other side of my desk. "Is there anything in Scripture about people being responsible
for their own plants and animals?" she asked. "I
know that the Old Testament has lots of rules
about sheep and goats and whose fields are whose.
But is there anything that might apply to my leaf
situation?"

Alvina informed me that Ollie Lundin had just
yesterday returned the oak leaves. "It took me
hours to rake and sort them and he just dumped
them back—in broad daylight, Pastor! And not
only his oak leaves, but quite a few of his maple
leaves, too." I was going to ask her how she knew
whose maple leaves were whose, but decided that

allest step into this legal thicket would be
...nd of me.

...he had been to see our police chief, Billy Ho-
...art, who, she complained, had been no help. He
had told her that there were no laws about whose
leaves were whose, which Alvina suggested was a
major legal oversight. "Everybody in town has always just sorta raked their own yards and not worried about whose tree the leaves came from," Billy
had said. But to Alvina it seemed patently unfair
that she, who had only one small maple in her
back yard, should be required to clean up the mess
made by other people's trees. She was growing
more adamant and animated and seemed to have
lost any trace of the reluctance I had noticed when
I came upon her doing what was "only fair" in the
middle of the night.

I was about ready to make the only point I
could think of—namely, that no mortal wisdom
could ever discern whose leaves were whose,
which was a sort of theological version of the line
Billy Hobart had tried—but Alvina guessed my direction and in the heat of righteous indignation
told me something I don't think she had planned
to reveal. She sat up even straighter in her chair
and said, "This past summer, I hired Danny Olson
to go up in my tree and mark my leaves. He put
an X on each one with a Magic Marker. Only took
him two days." This, she said, allowed her to tell
those maple leaves that were her responsibility
from everybody else's errant ones. She allowed
that the X's tended to fade and some were hard to

see. *Especially in the dark,* I thought to myself. Next year, she said, she would have Danny do it later in the summer.

A picture formed in my mind's eye: gangly fifteen-year-old Danny Olson with a Magic Marker in his hand, long legs wrapped around a branch as he tried to reach the leaves on the end. And I could see Alvina down on the ground pointing out the ones he'd missed: "Now, Danny, be sure to mark that bunch just below your left arm." I could not imagine that he had been able to come anywhere close to putting an X on every one of Alvina's leaves. He undoubtedly didn't mention to her that he might have missed a few. But even a hint of a chuckle at that moment and Alvina Johnson would slam the door in my face for the rest of her days or mine, whichever came first. In the end I had no biblical ammunition for her to aim at Ollie Lundin, who, she said, "was a Lutheran of some kind and would probably pay attention to Scripture."

Alvina is not happy with me, but she's not generally happy with anybody. I assume she and Ollie are going to go on dumping leaves over their fence for a while, and that Danny Olson will have a couple of days' work next summer. But what impressed me about my brief involvement in the Jefferson Street leaf war was Alvina's righteous appeal to what she kept calling "fair." There was simply no doubt in her mind that the ultimate ethic of the cosmos is what's "fair."

The only other people I know who talk as much

about what's fair and what's not fair are my children. And, like all parents, our predictable response to their predictable lament that something isn't "fair," is to say, "Get used to it; the world's not fair." But their faith in "fairness" as the moral yardstick of the universe remains unshaken. Which is as it should be. Fairness is the ethic of adolescence. My hope is that their present zeal for fairness will make them fair in the way they treat other people the rest of their lives. When they were small children they believed that they were quite obviously the center of creation and that all things existed only to please them. They are growing beyond that now, thank God. But some people never do.

In time, I hope that they will also grow beyond the ethic of fairness—not that they leave it behind, but that they come to see that it is not the end of wisdom. Fairness is what the law tries to write down and, like the law, it is absolutely necessary. But it will fall short in the end, for it cannot make all things right and good.

This is what old Jeremiah was hinting at in chapter 31 when he ruminated about a new covenant and a law written on hearts. The old law had simply been unable to form people into the crucible of love and justice that he knew God wanted. It had demanded only an outward conformity. But the prophet dreamed of an inward fire. That fire is gracious love and it lies beyond what's merely fair.

It isn't fair, I suppose, that Alvina, who has one small maple tree, has to rake a lot of leaves from the Lundins' trees. It's not fair, but it would be a gracious thing for her to do.

Hunting

Winter has come early to the northern plains. The fall—nobody here uses the eastern word, autumn—was a lovely time, short as it was, a gentler than usual season of warmish diamond-clear days and cool nights. On many an evening Annie and I sat on the front porch in heavy coats with hot coffee and breathed air that became wet and heavy as the temperature dropped, smelling rich and fecund with fallen leaves and the dying impatiens at either side of the front stoop.

The fall here is no riot of color. The islands of cottonwood, maples, and box elders turn to yellows and browns, but the surrounding sea of soybean and field corn dominates the landscape. And that rolling ocean becomes a brown stubble against the oil-black of the dirt. Brown and black are the colors of fall here. It is lovely, but no one here would think of driving around just to look at it.

The fall is given over to three activities: canning fruits and vegetables for women, hunting for men, and high school football for everybody. I suppose it has been this way from the dim mists of human history. Primitive adolescent males played violent and daring games of some sort while adolescent females watched; the women of the clan gathered nuts, berries, and roots and salted or dried them for the famine of winter; the men and older boys, armed with clubs and flint-tipped spears, chased down now extinct species of deer, and maybe in a good year a woolly mammoth.

Not much has changed in twenty thousand years. The adolescent game is now horribly complicated and requires expensive equipment, the women have self-sealing Ball jars, and the men have traded in their spears for shotguns. With four-wheel-drive pickup trucks, they don't need to run as fast or as far as their ancestors did in the hunt, if they have to run at all.

With each one of these ancient activities there still comes a certain camaraderie. The kids talk football, and so do many of their parents. Together they remember great plays and notable victories of years past. They shake their heads and click their tongues and say, "Yeh, yeh, that sure was some catch Donnie made." Women talk canning at the church coffee hour: "Alice, did you know Piggly Wiggly's got eight-ounce Ball jars on sale?" And the men talk hunting. They tell the same stories again and again, stories grown with the years to be even better than the truth was: "I tell ya, Bill, I could hear that ten-point buck snortin', I was that close. Scared the piss out of me when he bolted."

My wife and I have stood apart from most of this over the years we've been here. As children of the sixties and of the suburbs it was foreign to us, as well as unapologetically sexist. Anyway, church members load us up with more canned peaches, strawberry jam, and wild duck than we can eat. Even this, I suppose, shadows the ancient days when the members of the clan left such offerings at the opening of the cave of the tribe's shaman and his woman.

So I was at a loss for words last Sunday when Jimmy Wilcox came up to me in the greeting line after church and invited me to go hunting with him. Jimmy's my age, a native who never left town. He runs the local oil heat business. He's always been something of a thorn in my flesh, vaguely adversarial without being confrontational. When he was on Session, it seemed as though every other sentence out of his mouth began "Well . . . I dunno . . ." I've always suspected an unconscious rivalry in him, a resentment toward me, the guy from the Outside World with (what seems to him) a fancy education and smooth ways.

I was so taken aback at this invitation that I could not find the right words with which to say "no" before he went on to explain that the particular hunt he was proposing was one that even I, "a man of the cloth"—there was the barest provocative edge to those words—would not find objectionable. "You hearda fishin' where you throw 'em all back," he said. "Well, this is huntin' where you can throw 'em all back if ya want."

I felt a hand on my shoulder and turned to see old Angus MacDowell, who gave me just a bit of a squeeze below the neck and said, "C'mon, David. Do ya good." Now I have a deep affection for this man, outwardly stiff, but inwardly a still well of quiet grace.

Curious and a bit flattered to be included, I started to open my mouth to ask the obvious questions about how you could "throw 'em back." Before I could get a word out, Angus let go of my neck and gave me a sharp slap on the back and said, "Good, it's all settled then. We'll pick ya up Friday a week, five at night." And they rushed out the front door with uncharacteristic suddenness. I turned back to the greeting line vaguely bewildered by it all. Alvina Johnson found my hand, shook it vigorously, and said, "Nice sermon, Revrunt."

By the time I got home I was beyond curious; I was intrigued. Perhaps is was some racial memory of man against beast buried in the back of my brain. Perhaps it was a sense that my inclusion was a rite of passage that would initiate me into the local fellowship of men. Maybe it was simply a longing for adventure nursed by a life of routine. Whatever it was, by dinnertime I was on the edge of excited. Something in me longed for the hunt. I was less sure how I might inform my family of this impending and mysterious expedition. I decided on nonchalance with my wife. I found an L.L. Bean catalogue in the magazine rack and idly flipped through it as she mashed the potatoes.

"You know, I could use one of these camouflage vests when I go hunting with Jimmy Wilcox." She stopped mashing and looked at me incredulously: "Hunting! With Jimmy Wilcox! You?!"

Jennifer, our thirteen-year-old, was even less subtle. Having been weaned on Bambi and brought up watching "Wild Kingdom," she had developed into something of an adolescent animal-rights activist. She was the neighborhood's protector of stray cats and guardian of unloved dogs. A week before my invitation to hunt we had been driving to Mankato together when we met a car with the carcass of a white-tailed deer roped to the left front fender. "Neanderthals!" she cried out in horror and indignation as the car flashed by. I had been impressed with the word "Neanderthal." A week later, when she shouted it at me for planning to go hunting with Jimmy and Angus, I grew defensive. I dragged out the old argument about hunting being every bit as humane as the process that gave her the hamburgers and fried chicken she so enjoyed.

The day of the hunt—the Friday after Thanksgiving—arrived cold and sharp. About noon I called Angus up to ask him how I ought to dress and what I needed to bring. "Nuthin', Dave, nuthin'. Just dress good and warm, but no bright-colored clothes. We got all the stuff." At ten minutes after five, Jimmy drove up in his blue Chevy Blazer 4 × 4. Annie kissed her man farewell and made the only comment about the hunt since the mashed potatoes. She patted me on the chest of my just-arrived L.L. Bean camouflage vest and said, "Go bring back plenty meat to cave for woman to cook," and pushed me out the door.

Jimmy had the heater in the Blazer blasting away as we drove out of town to the south. They eyed my new vest without comment, though I thought I detected a wry smile on Angus's lips when he saw it. But I felt a man among men, off to do things that men do and have done since the beginning.

It was Angus who broke the close silence and answered my bursting curiosity. "Too late for ducks, Dave. Not many pheasant this year, so we're gonna hunt snipe."

"Snipe?" I asked.

"Ya, snipe," Angus replied. "Huntin' snipe is a different kinda deal. They're nocturnal, you know." He hesitated and then added, "They only come out at night. So ya can't shoot 'em. I mean, ya can't see 'em to shoot 'em, so ya gotta catch 'em by usin' their natural instincts."

Angus then explained the details of the night's hunt. "This is their natural mating season, late fall. The males and the females find each other by their call, their snipe call. Now, ya see, the snipe call sounds for all the world like two sticks bein' hit together. When a snipe hears that sound, he just runs hell-bent for the source of it. Which is how you hunt 'em."

The Blazer pulled off the highway and onto a dirt road that led to an unused airfield, another failed attempt to put North Haven on the map.

"This place has always been good for snipe," Larry casually observed. We climbed out and Jimmy opened the tailgate and pulled out the hunting equipment—half a dozen gunnysacks and a couple of stripped green ash sticks about a foot and a half long. He turned to me, put his finger to his lips, and said, "From now on, we all gotta be real quiet." Angus and I nodded in agreement as we set off across the overgrown field to the edge of a recently harvested cornfield on the other side.

Once there, Angus said, "Me and Jimmy are gonna be the beaters; you're gonna be the catcher, Dave. You stay here and do this." He knelt as if he were about to pray and continued, "You get on your knees and you put this gunnysack between your knees and keep it open by tucking the top edge into your belt. Then you hit the sticks together like so." Angus tapped the two hickory sticks rapidly: "Tap, tap," and then rubbed the one along the other to make a soft, grating sound. "You got that, Dave, tap, tap, rub; tap, tap, rub. To a snipe it sounds just like another snipe ready and waiting. You just keep that up and me and Jimmy will go back across the field and see if we can drive 'em to ya. Now, when they come, they're gonna come real sudden, they're gonna come outa nowhere like a bullet, and if you're lucky, right between your legs and into the gunnysack. Then ya just tie up the top of the sack and grab another one and wait for the next taker."

I had seen stranger things than this on "Wild Kingdom." I dropped to my knees and fixed the gunnysack to my belt to keep it open. Jimmy started stuffing cornstalks into my L.L. Bean vest —to give me better cover, he explained. After the beaters were out of sight, I began: tap, tap, rub; tap, tap, rub. And I waited, sensing excitedly any number of times that there was movement out there in the field and that at any moment one of these bullet-like birds would dash out of the darkness and into my sack.

By seven-thirty, I was shivering with the cold. My knees ached from contact with the frozen earth. The cornstalks stuffed down my back were itching my ears and the "tap, tap, rub" was wearing on me. It was then that I heard from across the field the unmistakable sound of two car doors being shut quietly, but not quite quietly enough. An agonizing revelation swept over me. My beaters weren't out in the field driving the snipe toward me; they'd been sitting in the Blazer for the last two hours drinking coffee. And there were no snipe, and even if there were I wasn't going to catch them with a gunnysack between my legs beating two sticks together, which I was still doing as all this came to me.

"Fool," I said out loud to myself, "perfect fool. You're forty-one years old, you've got a bachelor's degree in English, a master's in Divinity, you've studied Greek and Hebrew and you've been to London and Paris, and here you are on your knees with a sack between your legs, rubbing two sticks together waiting for a bird to fly in."

So I stopped tap, tap, rubbing, pulled the cornstalks out of my vest, and sat back on the other five gunnysacks. I felt my face go red-hot with anger and embarrassment. I heard a rustle behind me and turned to see Angus coming up alongside me. "Catch anything, David?" I couldn't answer. He lowered his eighty-five-year-old bones down beside me on the gunnysacks and proceeded to tell the story of the time sixty years ago an army buddy took him snipe hunting. He described his feelings when he realized after nearly three hours in the snow on the edge of a cornfield that there were no snipe to be caught. And he turned to me and looked me in the eyes and he laughed and laughed as I'd never heard the old man laugh. He took me by the shoulders and shook me as he laughed until I could do nothing but join in a duet of stupid laughter.

And so I laughed till I nearly cried, which told Jimmy that it was safe to come out of the dark. He stepped toward us and sat down on his haunches and told the story of his snipe hunt. He then passed around a flask of schnapps, and we each took a slug. Sitting there in the cold on the gunnysack I felt a kinship with these men, each of them very different from me. I could never have imagined this before we went snipe hunting together. The hunting forced me to my knees and led me into the ancient fellowship of fools, the camaraderie of the humbled. It was a community that those who guard their pride too closely never know. And so I looked at Angus and said, "You know, my brother's coming for Christmas, and I don't believe he's ever been snipe hunting."

Rapture

Thanksgiving is simply too late in the year, perched on the brink of December, breathing down the back of Christmas. It's too late to be a proper harvest festival, unless you're a rice farmer in Louisiana or a Florida orange grower. We come to church in late November and sing, "All is safely gathered in, ere the winter storms begin." Well, it was all safely gathered in at least six weeks ago and the first winter storms generally roll out of the Dakotas in early November. Last year, in fact, the winter storms began ere all was safely gathered in when it hailed and snowed the third week of September.

About half the folks in this church are from farm families and last year they had to look hard for what they might give thanks for on the fourth Thursday in November. Some folks said they didn't come to church on that Sunday before Thanksgiving because they were too tired or feeling a bit peaked. But in truth, they didn't come because they were angry—angry at the worry, the endless work, angry at the hail and the snow, angry at being broke, and—deep, deep down—angry at God. But they don't believe that it's all right to be angry with God, even for a moment, so on Thanksgiving Sunday they decide to feel poorly, which avoids an uncomfortable meeting with the Author of Providence until their anger passes.

Hazel Hofer was one such person. Hazel was newly widowed the day of the September snow when Anton went out to shovel a path to the barn and had a heart attack. He was only sixty-seven and had big plans. He had done well in the recent hard years and had bought out two flat-broke neighboring farmers. Just the summer before he had put up three new Butler storage units for all the field corn he expected to harvest. He was always getting ready to add a few acres, lease a bigger combine, or drain the wet spot that never yielded what it should. He was a good farmer, and usually a lucky one. Anton's master plan was to sell out to some agribusiness and move to Florida when he was seventy. The day after he died, I went to see Hazel. There was a rush of tears. Then she dried her eyes, looked squarely at me, and said, "He always had a plan for everything." She hiccuped a little laugh and added, "But not for this." She shed more tears and asked me whether I thought she should still go to Florida or stay on the farm. I told her not to decide anything important for a few months.

As I climbed into my car, I saw looming through the salt-smeared windshield Anton's three shiny new Butler storage units. I thought of the story in Luke's Gospel about the rich man whose land brought forth plentifully and who built bigger barns and sat back in self-satisfaction and said to his soul, "Soul, you have ample goods laid up for many years; take your ease, eat, drink, be merry" (i.e., buy a condo in Fort Lauderdale). But then God says (as He still often does), "Fool! This night your soul is required of you; and the things you have prepared, whose will they be?"

Well, in this case, they were all going to be Hazel's, who could have cared less. She had been to Florida and thought that it was too hot and even flatter than Minnesota. She never really wanted to move, but Anton had always planned on it. I put the car in reverse and tucked the seed of a sermon away to germinate.

It was the week before Thanksgiving Sunday that I went looking for that seed. Precisely how this story of a prosperous farmer snatched preemptively from his prosperity might grow into a Thanksgiving sermon in a lean year in southwestern Minnesota was a mystery to me. On Thursday, Arlene, our volunteer church secretary, put "Luke 12:15–24" on the mimeograph stencil and asked me what the sermon title was going to be. I said, "Give Thanks All the Days of Your Life." That would certainly cover anything I might say.

The sermon never got written, much less preached. Thursday night I was struck down with the flu: the shakes, headache, sore throat, and then every preacher's dread plague—laryngitis. By

Friday noon I could only croak monosyllables, like "Vicks." It was as though Divine Wisdom had foreknowledge (even before I had the knowledge) of what I was going to say on Sunday and decided to strike me dumb.

There was only one thing to do, unfortunately, and that was to call on the only spare preacher in a radius of fifty miles who would climb into a pulpit on such short notice: the Reverend Mr. Lex Ardent. He is a retired clergyman who spent his working days as an evangelist on what was left of the old Sawdust Trail, the tent meeting preaching circuit that is the ancestor of television ministry. His church is called the Apostolic Church of the Divine Christ in God, which broke off from a splinter group of a sect whose name includes all the same words somehow arranged in a different sequence.

I knew Lex through the local clergy association. He moved here when he retired six years ago to live with his son, Reg. Lex's theology had been strongly influenced by the woollier and more wild-eyed of the Old Testament prophets and their thunderings against idolatry, corruption, and all sins of the flesh. From this point in the Bible, Lex's religious thinking did a graceless leap over the Gospels and landed squarely in the Book of Revelation.

It was well known in town that Lex only preaches one sermon. He had gotten away with this over his forty-five-year career in itinerant evangelism because he had been forever moving from one tent meeting to the next. If the Sawdust Trail happened to bring him back to the same town again, Lex believed that a person who had been saved by his sermon the first time through would not need to be present the second time around. If someone did return, the sermon must not have worked the first time and he could well stand to hear it again.

Lex's lone sermon was about the Rapture, that esoteric doctrine beloved by those of an apocalyptic spirit. This doctrine says that at the Second Coming of Christ, all true and faithful followers (liberally numbered at 144,000) will be plucked live and whole from wherever they happen to be at that unexpected moment and whisked into the Kingdom. On the rear of his rusty Buick LeSabre Lex has a bumper sticker that says: IN CASE OF RAPTURE, DRIVER WILL DISAPPEAR. That bumper sticker is the core of Lex's theology and pretty much the whole point of his sermon.

In the sermon, Lex paints a dozen verbal pictures of people gathered together in various places, from which one of them—always only one—would suddenly and without warning disappear: people are waiting in line at the supermarket, and all of the sudden the checkout girl is gone—the Rapture! Kids sitting in school and, without a hint of what is to come—a seventh grader in the second row vanishes—the Rapture! Folks are shopping at Sears and suddenly the guy standing in the auto parts line is simply gone, leaving behind him the two brand-new snow tires he'll no

longer be needing—the Rapture! Then, in darker
tones sharpened over the years to a sinister edge,
Lex would describe a church service: worshipers
gathered on a Sunday morning, and only ONE of
them is "Raptured," actually hinting that the one
may not have been the preacher.

In this school of preaching, Lex is a master: he
launches his sermon slowly and quietly and then
climbs gradually into sermonic frenzy. It is, of
course, designed to scare the bejabbers out of his
listeners, most of whom on brief self-evaluation
count themselves among "Those Left Behind," as
Lex names them. Now that he was off the Sawdust
Trail and on the Substitute Preacher Circuit, Lex
has developed a knack for adapting the sermon to
any and every occasion. If it's a Christmas sermon,
he brings his listeners back down by ending with
something like "It was to save us from being left
behind that God sent Jesus to be born." If it's an
Easter sermon, he says, "It was to save us from
being left behind that God raised Christ from the
dead."

When Lex preached his sermon to Second Presbyterian on Thanksgiving Sunday, I was there, being too ill and mute to preach myself, but not sick
enough to stay home in bed. Frankly, I was a bit
curious as to how in the world Lex would work
his sermon around Thanksgiving. I underesti-
mated him. He found, of course, the text I had
already chosen from Luke very much to his liking.
"Good choice of Scripture, Dave. Good choice."

The day found Lex in fine form. As he

preached, he wandered away from the pulpit, waved his hands about, and pointed theatrically in the direction of the ceiling. He has no need for notes after all these years. Lex worked slowly into his great crescendo, jabbing at the heavens with both index fingers, painting pictures of lukewarm Sunday-only Christians with disappointed looks on their faces as they watched the few and the true swept up in the Rapture. All of this was a great novelty to the politely attentive congregation of Presbyterians, who rarely let themselves get swept up in anything, much less such rhetoric. After twenty-five minutes of this, Lex ended his sermon by slicing the air with his fingers, closing his eyes, and fairly shouting, "Thank God, thank God, in this season of Thanksgiving, thank God that it is not too late for anyone in this room!"

When he sat down, he looked exhausted. This was work for a younger man. Sweat was pouring down his temples. He pulled out a handkerchief and mopped his brow. Then he closed his eyes, threw his head back, and stretched his legs out in front of him. Lex had told me he liked the sermon to be the last thing in the service, except for a closing hymn. He fairly struggled to his feet to sing it, pushing himself up from the big mahogany preacher's chair. His eyes were still half closed, as though he had not yet descended from his hermeneutical high. Lex had picked the hymn "Come, Lord, and Tarry Not." We'd never sung it before, so most of the sound was coming from the direction of the choir: "Come, Lord, and tarry not; Bring the longed-for day; O why these years of waiting here, These ages of delay?"

Our choir, eight ladies and one gentleman, recesses out of the church during the closing hymn. We have no center aisle and if they were to go out via one of the two side aisles, they'd find themselves going out the front doors and into twenty-degree weather. So they leave the choir loft, which is up front on the left, march across the back of the chancel behind the communion table and out the right rear door, into the Westminster Room, and head straight for the coffeepot.

This is a direct but narrow path with one hazard —a wooden heating grate in the floor directly behind the big oak communion table. The grate measures two and a half feet square. It is made of pine and is just set in the hole in the floor that opens to the heating duct below. The duct bends at a right angle about three feet down before continuing on to the old hot-air furnace.

Emma Bowers, a soprano, is new to the choir. She is a small woman and gives herself another three inches of height by wearing those spiked high-heeled shoes that faded from fashion twenty years ago. As she passed over the heating grate that Sunday morning, her right heel went into one of the little square holes and lodged there tight. The processing choir, hymnbooks in front of their faces and open to page 233, slowed as Emma tugged to free her foot. I guess the shoes were old and tight. Her shoe stayed on and the heel didn't break off. On her third and mighty pull, Emma lifted the whole grate (which wasn't so heavy) right out of the duct and moved on, trooper that she is, walking as if she'd been shot in the leg but was trying not to notice.

Right behind her was Elsie Johnson, Alvina's younger sister by ten years, who, to put it kindly, does not have a keen awareness of her immediate environment. She can see all right; she just never seems to notice things. I turned to see if Lex had noticed Emma plowing along, determined to make it to the rear door as if nothing at all had happened.

He looked over to watch just as Elsie Johnson stepped to where the grate wasn't. She gave a little squealing "Whoop!" and just disappeared from sight behind the communion table.

Lex dropped his jaw in a flabbergasted gape. His eyes went wide, his hymnbook slipped from his hand, and then he shut his eyes tight: THE RAPTURE! Still in the grip of his sermonic euphoria, he saw before his very eyes the scene he had been putting in words for forty-five years. Elsie had been taken and he was left behind. This state of flabbergasted misapprehension lasted for perhaps four seconds. I am sure it was the longest four seconds in Lex's life.

Then his look shifted from horror to befuddlement to immense relief. He closed his eyes and mouthed what was surely a prayer of earnest thanksgiving that the Apocalypse was delayed.

Elsie hadn't even fallen over, but rather stepped square into the duct and went down the three feet to where it turns horizontal. There wasn't a scratch on her, and to this day, I'm not sure that she's clear as to just what happened. A dozen people ran to her rescue. They fished her out and dusted her off. After things quieted down I stood up and croaked, "She's okay," and then whispered a hoarse benediction.

I went home exhausted, ate a whole bag of potato chips, and went to bed. About eight o'clock that evening I awoke feeling much better. The worst of the flu aches were passed and my mental picture of those four seconds in Lex's life were becoming a great joy to me. I remembered my reason for choosing those words from Luke in the first place—Anton Hofer, who had put up three new Butler bins one day and was gone the next. I saw Elsie vanishing with a "Whoop!" and thought of all the dear hearts who have vanished just as suddenly from my sight: my grandparents, some older uncles, a friend from seminary.

I took a shower and put on my bathrobe and looked at myself in the mirror. I imagined myself vanishing into the floor with a "Whoop!" and said to my soul: "Soul, You haven't got a thing in any storehouse: no bank account, you don't even own the house you live in. You have no silo to put silage in, but here you are, graying and getting lumpy. You might never have been. You have no right to have been, but here you are."

I went in to kiss our six-year-old Christopher good night. He was only half asleep, and pulled me down beside him with little arms and big love.

I crawled into his bed as he fell into child sleep. I could hear his breathing, his mouth open, and feel his heart beating, his chest pulled tight against my side. He might not have been, but he is.

And lying there all fell into place: the early snow and the lost crops, my flu and the near-disaster in church that morning—all of this is as nothing when set next to the gratuitous gift of life here and now. This is indeed the day the Lord has made. Let us rejoice and be glad in it.

Christmas Baptism

Annie and the kids and I have come at last to be at home in this little town once unknown and unimaginable to us. Even so, that honeymoon between the pastor and the congregation is long since past as witnessed by events that began to unfold the Sunday before Thanksgiving.

In coffee hour after the worship service, a taciturn, silver-haired pillar of the congregation named Angus MacDowell informed me that his son, Larry, and Larry's wife, Sherry, who live in Spokane, Washington, would be visiting for the Thanksgiving weekend. Sherry, it seems, had just presented the MacDowell clan with a son, named, believe it or not, Angus Larry. However, Angus informed me, they were planning on calling him Skip, which name Skip's grandfather spat disdainfully out of his mouth. Since they were going to be in town and since Sherry's folks just live in Mankato and since this was going to be a big reunion, they wanted me to "do the baby," as Angus put it, next Sunday.

I got Angus out of coffee hour and into my study for an informal discussion about the integrity of the sacrament of baptism, which is what I assumed he meant by "doing the baby." I asked Angus about Larry and Sherry's church affiliation in Spokane, explaining that it was best for a child to be baptized in the church where he would be raised. It seems, though, that they had not yet settled on a church that they liked, though they'd been there nine years. I talked about the importance of the parents' commitment to the faith and the fact that they are asked to make some rather sweeping and deep promises in the course of it all. Angus soon caught my drift: Larry and Sherry ought to find a church home out in Spokane and have Skip baptized there.

Angus listened to all this in a rather dignified and formal silence. He offered no response, much less argument. He simply rose without a word, shook my hand, and thanked me for my time. Fool that I was, I thought that the matter was settled. Angus is an elder of the church and one of that dwindling breed of courtly, gentle, but inflexibly stiff patriarchs of the church.

In my experience, they seem to wear nothing but dark blue serge suits, a sort of uniform identifying them as members of an army in defense of the status quo. I remember encountering a whole flock of these blue-suited elders some twenty-five years ago on the day I was set before the church board to be examined for my confirmation. They were seated around a long, dark mahogany table in the church board room, eight or ten of them, all in their dark blue suits and me, a skinny little thirteen-year-old in a corduroy jacket with sleeves three inches too short. They welcomed me, and then one of them, the one with wire-rimmed glasses, asked me my prearranged question from the catechism: "What is effectual calling?" I had been practicing the answer, which I can still recite, for three months, but something about his look and the way he emphasized the word "effectual" threw me off balance. I almost wet my pants. I believe I then gave the answer for the question "What is predestination?" They confirmed me anyway, not out of mercy, but because I was thirteen and when you were thirteen and from a Presbyterian family, you were confirmed. They were hardly going to permit my fogginess on predestination and effectual calling to alter tradition. Serge-suited elders are a resolute and determined lot.

True to his type, after Angus left my office, he simply spoke with all the members of the board about a special meeting to approve the baptism of Angus Larry. They had the meeting, asked me to please stop by, and voted 9–0 in favor of the baptism. So on the morning of the Sunday after Thanksgiving, we "did" little Angus Larry. This congregation has an odd little baptismal custom: the pastor, I was gently informed when we first came here, always asks, "Who stands with this child?" and then the whole extended family of the little one rises and remains standing for the ceremony. So, Angus Larry in my arms, I asked, "Who stands with this child?" and up stood Angus in his blue serge suit and his wife, Minnie, and Sherry's folks from Mankato and a couple of cousins.

After church, everybody rushed home to turkey leftovers and I went back into the sanctuary to turn off the lights. A middle-aged woman, dressed Salvation Army style, was sitting in the front pew with a black plastic purse in her lap. I knew her as someone who always sat in the very last pew, as close to a door as possible, but I did not know her name. She seemed at a loss for words and was hesitant about looking at me for very long. She finally said her name was Mildred Cory and commented as to how lovely the baptism was. After another long pause she said that her daughter, Tina, had just had a baby and, well, the baby ought to be baptized, shouldn't it?

I suggested that Tina and her husband should call me and we would discuss the appropriateness of baptism. Mildred hesitated again, and then catching and holding my eyes for the first time, said, "Tina's got no husband; Tina's just eighteen and she was confirmed in this church four years ago. She used to come out for the Senior High Fellowship, but then she had started to see this older boy out of high school." She hesitated for a moment, gathered her courage, and let the rest of the story tumble out fearlessly: "Then she got pregnant and decided to keep the baby and she wants to have it baptized here in her own church, but she's nervous to come and talk to you, Reverend. She's named the baby James," she said, "Jimmy." I said that I would bring the request to the church board for approval.

When the matter came up at the meeting, there was a moot question or two about why in the world Tina Cory was keeping the baby. I had started to explain what everybody already knew, namely that Tina was a member of the church, an unwed mother, and that I didn't know who the father was. They all knew who the father was, of course. This is a small town. The father was young Jimmy Hawthorne, who had recently chosen a career in his nation's armed forces and was now completing basic training at Fort Bragg. A few questions were asked as to whether we could be certain that Tina would stick to the commitment she was making in having her child baptized. The Angus Larry affair had set me in a feisty mood and I remarked that she and little Jimmy were, after all, right here in town where we could give them support. I did not have to say, "and not in Spokane"; they all thought it.

The real problem was the picture of the baptism that we all had in our heads: Tina, pimples on her chin, little Jimmy in her arms, big Jimmy long fled to North Carolina, and Mildred Cory the only one who would stand when the question was asked. It hurt to think of it, but they approved it, of course. The baptism was scheduled for the last Sunday in Advent.

The church was full, as it always is the Sunday before Christmas. The rumored snow had not yet come, though the sky was heavy with it. After the sermon, the elder who was to assist me in the baptism stood up beside me at the baptismal font and read the words I had written out on a three-by-five card: "Tina Cory presents her son for baptism." He kept looking at the card and not at Tina, who was rising to come forward, as if there was some further point he wished to make.

Down the aisle she came, nervously, briskly, smiling at me only, shaking slightly with month-old Jimmy in her arms, a blue pacifier stuck in his mouth. The scene hurt, all right, every bit as much as we all knew it would. So young this mother was, and so alone. One could not help but remember another baby boy born long ago to a young and unwed mother in difficult circumstances.

I read the opening part of the service, noting Mildred Cory sitting strangely out of place in a front pew. Then I asked, "Who stands with this child?" I nodded at Mildred slightly to coax her to her feet. She rose slowly, looking to either side, and then returned my smile.

My eyes went back to my service book. I was just about to ask Tina the parents' questions of commitment when I became aware of movement in the pews. Angus MacDowell had stood up in his blue serge suit, Minnie beside him. Then a couple of other elders stood up, then the sixth-grade Sunday school teacher stood up, then a new young couple in church, and soon, before my incredulous eyes, the whole church was standing up with little Jimmy. Tina was crying, of course, and Mildred Cory was holding on to the pew in front of her as though she was standing on the deck of a ship rolling in a great wind, which, in a way, she was.

The unexpectedness of this departure from the routine at first disquieted but then quieted us all, even little Jimmy, who had been wiggling and squeaking as though he might be preparing to screech. As the water touched his forehead, he seemed almost to focus his infant senses. The water rolled back into the thin wisps of baby hair, down the bridge of his nose, and onto his cheek. His eyes looked to the side as though he were concentrating on something. Every eye was on the child, who was for a moment everybody's baby. I broke my gaze and looked up to the congregation to let them know I was about to offer the baptismal prayer. I noticed Angus straining to see Jimmy from three pews back. The old man was looking into the infant face with an openmouthed smile that surely remembered his own baby, now a grown man with a baby of his own.

The Scripture reading that morning had been some verses from 1 John: "See what great love the Father has given us that we should be called children of God . . . No man has ever seen God; if we love one another, God abides in us and his love is perfected in us . . . there is no fear in love, but perfect love casts out fear." In that baptism, those old words came alive. They were clothed in flesh and everybody saw it.

Michael Lindvall was born in 1947 in Minnesota into a tradition of what he likes to call "straight-backed Scandinavian piety." His family moved from town to town over the entire state and into the Upper Peninsula of Michigan, settling in such places as Pierz, Red Lake Falls, Willmar, White Bear Lake, and Manistique—all of which he calls "wonderfully sane little communities that love to tell and retell good stories." He then went on to study at the universities of Wisconsin and Michigan and decided along the way to become a minister. After finishing at Princeton Theological Seminary, he worked as an associate pastor of a church in Detroit and has since 1979 been the pastor of the First Presbyterian Church of Northport, New York, a town on the North Shore of Long Island. The congregation there has heard many of these stories before as Michael Lindvall's sermons at a Sunday service. He lives in Northport with his wife Terri and his children Madeline, Benjamin, and Grace.